Herbert S. Stone and Company

Essays from the Chap-book

Being a miscellany of curious and interesting Tales, Histories, etc.

Herbert S. Stone and Company

Essays from the Chap-book

Being a miscellany of curious and interesting Tales, Histories, etc.

ISBN/EAN: 9783337073626

Printed in Europe, USA, Canada, Australia, Japan

Cover: Foto ©ninafisch / pixelio.de

More available books at **www.hansebooks.com**

ESSAYS
from the
Chap-Book

BEING A *MISCELLANY* OF
Curious and interefting Tales,
Hiftories, &c; *newly com-
pofed by* MANY CELE-
BRATED WRITERS
and very delight-
ful to read.

CHICAGO.
Printed for *Herbert S. Stone & Company,*
and are to be fold by them at *The
Caxton Building* in *Dearborn Street*
1896

COPYRIGHT, 1896, BY
HERBERT S. STONE & CO.

CONTENTS

BOYESEN, H. H.   PAGE
   IBSEN'S NEW PLAY 5
BURROUGHS, JOHN
   BITS OF CRITICISM 19
DEKOVEN, MRS. REGINALD
   VERLAINE: A FEMININE APPRECIATION . 27
EARLE, ALICE MORSE
   DEGENERATION 37
   THE PLEASURES OF HISTORIOGRAPHY . . 47
   THE BUREAU OF LITERARY REVISION . . 59
GATES, LEWIS E.
   MR. MEREDITH AND HIS AMINTA . . . 67
GOSSE, EDMUND
   THE POPULARITY OF POETRY 89
GUINEY, LOUISE IMOGEN
   CONCERNING ME AND THE METROPOLIS . 101
   "TRILBY" 109
HAPGOOD, NORMAN
   MODERN LAODICEA 119
   THE INTELLECTUAL PARVENU 129

HIGGINSON, THOMAS WENTWORTH PAGE
    THE SCHOOL OF JINGOES 141
JERROLD, LAURENCE
    THE USES OF PERVERSITY 149
MABIE, HAMILTON WRIGHT
    A COMMENT ON SOME RECENT BOOKS . 157
    ONE WORD MORE 167
MOULTON, LOUISE CHANDLER
    THE MAN WHO DARES 177
SIMPSON, EVE BLANTYRE
    R. L. S. SOME EDINBURGH NOTES . . 195
STODDARD, RICHARD HENRY
    MR. GILBERT PARKER'S SONNETS . . . 209
THOMPSON, MAURICE
    IS THE NEW WOMAN NEW? 223
    THE RETURN OF THE GIRL 239
    THE ART OF SAYING NOTHING WELL . 253

Ibsen's New Play
By
H. H. Boyesen

IBSEN'S NEW PLAY.

NEVER has the great master written anything simpler and more human than "Little Eyolf." The two fundamental chords which sound with varying force through all his earlier works are here struck anew with increased distinctness and resonance. The ennobling power of suffering, the educational value of pain, — that is the first lesson which the play conveys ; and the second, which is closely akin to it, is the development of personality through the discipline of renunciation.

Alfred Allmers, a poor and obscure man of letters, has married Rita, a rich and beautiful heiress. During the first seven or eight years of their marriage they live frankly the life of the senses ; and in amorous intoxication forget the world with its claims, being completely absorbed in each other. Their little son Eyolf they leave largely to his aunt, Asta (Allmers's supposed sister), and only interest themselves in him spasmodically, and then to very little purpose.

Rita is, in fact, not very fond of the child, and feels vaguely annoyed whenever she is reminded of her duties toward it. It is directly due to her erotic intensity that the boy, who has been left in his highchair at table, tumbles down and is crippled for life. He then becomes a reproach to his mother, and she rather shuns than seeks the sight of him.

I find this development of Rita to be true and consistent. Women, as a rule, after marriage, develop the wifely character at the expense of the maternal, or the maternal at the expense of the wifely. Rita Allmers belongs to the former class. She is young, beautiful, and passionate; her wifehood is all to her; her motherhood only incidental. But this condition cannot endure. The husband, at all events, feels a subtle change steal over his relation to his wife; and in order to make it clear to himself, he goes on a long pedestrian tour into the mountains. On his return, at the end of two weeks, he is received by Rita with a bacchanalian seductiveness which ill befits his serious mood. He has resolved to introduce a radical change in the household. He will henceforth devote himself to the education of his son, and make that his chief concern. His book on "Human Responsibility," at which he has been writing in a desultory fashion, shall no longer divert his attention from the actual responsibility, which it were a sin to shirk. Rita, however, when he unfolds his plan to her, is anything but pleased. She wants him all to herself, and is not content to share him with anybody, even though it be her own child. She cannot be put off with crumbs of affection. She coaxes, she threatens; she hints at dire consequences. With the passionate vehemence of a spoiled and petted beauty, who believes her love disdained, she upbraids him, and cries out at last that she wishes the child had never been born. Presently a wild scream is heard from the pier, and little Eyolf's crutch is seen floating upon the still waters of the fiord.

The second act opens with a scene in which Asta is endeavoring to console Allmers in his affliction. He is trying to find the purpose, the meaning of his bereavement. "For there must be a meaning in it," he exclaims. "Life, existence, — destiny *cannot* be so utterly meaningless." Asta had loved the dead child, and he feels drawn to her by the communion of sorrow. From Rita, on the other hand, he feels repelled, because he cannot, in spite of her wild distraction, believe in the genuineness of her grief. She demands black crape, flag at half mast, and all the outward symbols of mourning; but the sensation which now is torturing her is not pain at the loss of the boy, but self-reproach. The keen tooth of remorse is piercing the very marrow of her bones. For the first time in her life she forgets how she looks, — what impression she is making. And that is, psychologically, a wholesome change. The centre of her consciousness is wrenched violently out of herself, and she sees existence with a different vision. A most admirable symbol for this unsleeping remorse which is stinging and scorching her conscience is "the great, open eyes" of little Eyolf, as he was seen lying on the bottom of the fiord. These eyes pursue the guilty mother. "They will haunt me all my life long," she declares. Keen, simple, and soul-searching is the conversation between husband and wife, as the first quiverings of a spiritual life are awakened in both of them under the lash of an accusing conscience. Even while they upbraid each other, each trying to shift his share of responsibility upon the other, a vague shame takes possession of them, and the guilty heart knows and avows its guilt. They conceive of Eyolf's death as a judgment upon them, as a retribution for their shirking their parental duty. For the first time in their lives they stand soul to soul in all their naked paltriness. It is scarcely strange that they should shrink from each other. But a new sincerity is born of the very futility of embellishing pretences. The secret thoughts which each has had of the other, but never has dared to utter, pop forth, like toads out of their holes, and show their ugly faces. His book, which Allmers had professed to regard as his great life-work, was, as Rita has long since guessed, a mere makeshift to give a spurious air of importance to his idleness, and he has abandoned it, not as a sacrifice to parental duty, but because he distrusted his ability to finish it. But when such things have been said — when each has stripped the other of all dissembling draperies — how is life to continue? How is their marriage to regain its former beauty and happiness? Alas, never! The old relation is definitely terminated and can never be renewed. It is because she feels this so deeply that Rita declares that henceforth she must have much company about her; for, she adds, "It will never do for Alfred and me to be alone." And Allmers, under the same profound revulsion of feeling, expresses his desire to separate from his wife. She wishes forgetfulness, and hopes to drown her remorse in social dissipations; while to him forgetfulness seems like disloyalty to the dead, and he determines to consecrate the future to his grief, with a dim idea that he may thus atone for his guilt. Being equally miserable alone or together, they turn in their despair to Asta and implore her to remain with them, and take the place of little Eyolf. But Asta, having discovered that Alfred is not her brother, is afraid to assume the dangerous rôle of consoler, and departs with the engineer Borgheim, who has long been in love with her.

In that dreary lethargy which follows violent grief, Rita and Allmers stand without the energy to readjust their lives to the changed conditions. The world is disenchanted for them; the very daylight beats upon their eyes with a brazen fierceness, and all things are empty, futile, devoid of meaning. But in the midst of this oppressive stillness new thoughts are born; new sentiments begin to stir. They are bound together, if by nothing else, by their communion in guilt. Their past memories and their common remorse constitute a bond which is scarcely less powerful than love. Very simply and patiently is the new birth of the spiritual life in both of them indicated in the following dialogue : —

ALLMERS — Yes, but you — you yourself — have bound me to you by our life together.

RITA — Oh, in your eyes I am not — I am not — entrancingly beautiful any more.

ALLMERS — The law of change may perhaps keep us together, none the less.

RITA (*Nodding slowly*) — There is a change in me now — I feel the anguish of it.

ALLMERS — Anguish ?

RITA — Yes, for change, too, is a sort of birth.

ALLMERS — It is — or a resurrection. Transition to a higher life.

RITA (*Gazing sadly before her*) — Yes, with the loss of all — all life's happiness.

ALLMERS — That loss is just the gain.

RITA — Oh, phrases ! Good heavens ! we are creatures of earth, after all.

ALLMERS — But something akin to the sea and the heavens, too, Rita.

Rita — You, perhaps; not I.

Allmers — Oh, yes — you, too; more than you suspect.

The force of the common memories asserts itself anew, and they resolve to remain together and help each other bear the burden of life. Death is no longer a horror, but a quiet fellow-traveller, neither welcomed nor dreaded. Very beautifully and naturally is the transition to the new altruistic endeavor indicated in their wonder why the little companions of Eyolf, who all could swim, made no effort to save him. Never had Eyolf's father and mother interested themselves in these boys; nor had they made the least effort to ameliorate the hard lot of the poor fishing population, settled about them. Having never sown love, they had never reaped it. Now, in order to fill the aching void of her heart with "something that is a little like love," Rita invites all the little ragamuffins from the village up into her luxurious house, clothes them in Eyolf's clothes, gives them Eyolf's toys to play with, and feeds them and warms them and lavishes upon them the homeless love which was her own child's due, but of which he was defrauded. In the opening up of this new well-spring of love in her heart, she suddenly perceives the meaning of Eyolf's death.

RITA — I suppose I must try if I cannot lighten — and ennoble their lot in life.

ALLMERS — If you can do that — then Eyolf was not born in vain.

RITA — Nor taken away from us in vain, either. . . . (*Softly, with a melancholy smile*) I want to make my peace with the great open eyes, you see.

ALLMERS (*Struck, fixing his eyes upon her*) — Perhaps I could join you in that? And help you, too, Rita?

And so they begin together a new existence, with new aims and a deeper sense of human responsibility. The contrast between the old life in the senses and the new life in the spirit, is emphasized in a few striking and simple phrases. Their aspiration is now consciously " upwards — towards the peaks, — towards the great silence."

"Little Eyolf," though its theme is closely akin to those of Ibsen's previous plays, is yet written in a new key, and it strikes in its conclusion a note which is quite alien to the author's earlier work. The declaration of human responsibility — in the sense of accountability, on the part of the refined and prosperous, for the degradation of the poor or miserable — sounds very strange upon his lips. If Carlyle at three score and ten had lifted up his voice and sung "The Song of the Shirt," or "The Cry of the Children," we could not have been more surprised. Ibsen's scorn of the nameless herd — of its meanness, its baseness, its purblind gropings and coarse enjoyments — rings loudly enough through "Peer Gynt," "The League of Youth," and "An Enemy of the People." What means this wonderful softening of his heart toward Nature's step-children, if not that his own vision has been enlarged, a new warm spring has been opened up in his old age, watering the roots of his being. It is obvious that in returning to his native land and becoming a world-renowned man, he has celebrated his reconciliation with humanity. The world is no longer so dark to him, nor destiny so cruel and meaningless as in the days of his obscurity. Very noble sound these mellow notes in the final scenes of "Little Eyolf," even though we miss occasionally the cadence of the harsh voice that spoke so many wholesome truths in "Brand" and "Rusmersholm." Interesting, too, it is to observe that the moral lesson of "Little Eyolf" is the very same as that of a score of Robert Browning's poems and dramas. Though Browning never emphasizes altruism to the extent that Ibsen does in the present play, the arousing of man, through suffering, from the life of the senses to that of the spirit is succinctly stated, the very soul of the Gospel according to Browning.

Bits of Criticism
By
John Burroughs

BITS OF CRITICISM

THE difference between a precious stone and a common stone is not an essential difference — not a difference of substance, but of arrangement of the particles — the crystallization. In substance the charcoal and the diamond are one, but in form and effect how widely they differ. The pearl contains nothing that is not found in the coarsest oyster-shell.

Two men have the same thoughts; they use about the same words in expressing them; yet with one the product is real literature, with the other it is a platitude.

The difference is all in the presentation; a finer and more compendious process has gone on in the one case than in the other. The elements are better fused and knitted together; they are in some way heightened and intensified. Is not here a clew to what we mean by style? Style transforms common quartz into an Egyptian pebble. We are apt to think of style as something external, that can be put

Bits of Criticism

on, something in and of itself. But it is not; it is in the inmost texture of the substance itself. Polish, choice words, faultless rhetoric, are only the accidents of style. Indeed, perfect workmanship is one thing; style, as the great writers have it, is quite another. It may, and often does, go with faulty workmanship. It is the use of words in a fresh and vital way, so as to give us a vivid sense of a new spiritual force and personality. In the best work the style is found and hidden in the matter.

I heard a reader observe, after finishing one of Robert Louis Stevenson's books, "How well it is written!" I thought it a doubtful compliment. It should have been so well written that the reader would not have been conscious of the writing at all. If we could only get the writing, the craft, out of our stories and essays and poems, and make the reader feel he was face to face with the real thing! The complete identification of the style with the thought; the complete absorption of the man with his matter, so that the reader shall say, "How good, how real, how true!" that is the great success. Seek ye the kingdom of truth first, and all things shall be added. I think we do feel, with regard to some of Stevenson's books, like "An Inland Voyage," "Travels with a Donkey," etc., how well they are written. Certainly one would not have the literary skill any less, but would have one's attention kept from it by the richness of the matter. Hence I think a British critic hits the mark when he says Stevenson lacks homeliness.

Dr. Holmes wrote fine and eloquent poems, yet I think one does not feel that he is essentially a poet. His work has not the inevitableness of nature; it is a skilful literary feat; we admire it, but seldom return to it. His poetry is a stream in an artificial channel; his natural channel is his prose; here we get his freest and most spontaneous activity.

One fault that I find with our younger and more promising school of novelists is that their aim is too literary; we feel that they are striving mainly for artistic effects. Do we feel this at all in Scott, Dickens, Hawthorne, or Tolstoi? These men are not thinking about art but about life; how to reproduce life. In essayists like Pater, Wilde, Lang, the same thing occurs; we are constantly aware of the literary artist; they are not in love with life, reality, so much as they are with words, style, literary effects. Their seriousness is mainly an artistic seriousness. It is not so much that they have something to say, as that they are filled with a desire to say something. Nearly all our magazine poets seem filled with the same desire; what labor, what art and technique; but what a dearth of feeling and spontaneity! I read a few lines or stanzas and then stop. I see it is only deft handicraft, and that the heart and soul are not in it. One day my boy killed what an old hunter told him was a mock duck. It looked like a duck, it acted like a duck, it quacked like a duck, but when it came upon the table — it mocked us. These mock poems of the magazines remind me of it.

Is it not unfair to take any book, certainly any great piece of literature, and deliberately sit down to pass judgment upon it? Great books are not addressed to the critical judgment, but to the life, the soul. They need to slide into one's life earnestly, and find him with his guard down, his doors open, his attitude disinterested. The reader is to give himself to them, as they give themselves to him; there must be self-sacrifice. We find the great books when we are young, eager, receptive. After we grow hard and critical we find few great books. A

CHAP-BOOK ESSAYS

By John Burroughs

recent French critic says: "It seems to me works of art are not made to be judged, but to be loved, to please, to dissipate the cares of real life. It is precisely by wishing to judge them that one loses sight of their true significance."

"How can a man learn to know himself?" inquires Goethe. "Never by reflection, only by action." Is not this a half-truth? One can only learn his powers of action by action, and his powers of thought by thinking. He can only learn whether or not he has power to command, to lead, to be an orator or legislator, by actual trial. Has he courage, self-control, self-denial, fortitude, etc.? In life alone can he find out. Action tests his moral virtues, reflection his intellectual. If he would define himself to himself he must think. "We are weak in action," says Renan, "by our best qualities; we are strong in action by will and a certain one-sidedness." "The moment Byron reflects," says Goethe, "he is a child." Byron had no self-knowledge. We have all known people who were ready and sure in action who did not know themselves at all. Your weakness or strength as a person comes out in action; your weakness or strength as an intellectual force comes out in reflection.

Verlaine: A Feminine
   Appreciation
By
Mrs. Reginald de Koven

VERLAINE: A FEMININE APPRECIATION

IN early days, when the triumphs and the torments of his overwhelming vitality swept at will across his soul, Paul Verlaine was sometimes god and sometimes satyr. From aspiring altitudes of spiritual emotions he swung like a pendulum to unspoken depths of vice.

The world spirit doubly charged his strange and terrible personality, pouring into it the essences and intuitions of the body and the soul. Into the alembic were dissolved the entities of Baudelaire and Villon, floating still upon the earth.

Then the whole was set to the vibration of a new rhythm as strange and as remote from the consciousness of men as the songs of inter-lunar space, so that his utterances with the naturalness of a bird's song or an infant's lisp should have the accents of melody undreamed of. And this is not all — strangest and most tragically terrible in its possibilities of pain — the chrism of conscience burns his sinister brow.

Verlaine: A Feminine Appreciation

The phantom of the immortal soul drives him into the outer darkness.

What are the undiscovered laws of spiritual heredity and of a poetic paternity, such as are suggested in the likeness of Baudelaire and Verlaine to their prototype Villon? The secret is yet to find. It is all as strange as the mystery of Bernhardt's strayed existence in this modern day. An emanation from some Egyptian tomb, wild spirit of geuius and of vice is she, vampire-like, inhuman, wandering among a people who have thrilled to her voice and wondered, not knowing whence she came.

Behind them both — Baudelaire with his luminous, despairing eyes, and Verlaine with his terrible glabrous head — the madcap figure of Villon shines out of a cloud of time, and we hear the sound of his reckless laughter and the music of his tears.

But if the relation between these two moderns and this singing renegade of the Middle Ages is that of mysterious paternity, between Baudelaire and Verlaine there is a brotherhood which is as wonderful as an oriental dream of metempsychosis.

Baudelaire's verses, read in early youth, so saturated and possessed the new-born soul of Paul Ver-

CHAP-BOOK ESSAYS

By Mrs. Reginald de Koven

laine that he became more a reincarnation of Baudelaire than a separate existence. The passions and the madness of Baudelaire became his own — he heard the same strange music — saw the same visions. Incarnate of the mad poet, Verlaine, his second soul, fled a second slave in the footsteps of the same strange goddess — beauty in decay.

And where one had madly followed, so the other fled, enamoured of her fatal loveliness, wherever her fickle steps should lead. Sometimes she would escape them, disappearing in mists and mysterious darkness, and sometimes they would come upon her suddenly in glimpses of green light, dancing strange frivolous steps, and the color of her robes would be mingled rose and mystic blue, and the halo of her head the phosphor of decay.

And she has led them through strange paths into the dwelling-place of death, and where love and life live together, for these two are never separated, and, through many places of terror and delight, to that ultimate spot, occult, remote, where dwells the soul of woman.

There the youngest of her slaves found himself one day outstripping his brother, and saw with living eyes the mystery, — and thenceforward he was no more Paul Verlaine; he was the prophet and interpreter of woman.

To him alone has the secret been revealed; to him alone, the mantle of deceit she wears, the slavish dress of the centuries, is no concealment. He has seen, has known, and he understands. "The very worst thing in the world," says an unknown writer, "is the soul of a woman." Forced to inaction, and fed on lies, her principal power, founded on man's weakness, curiosity, and the imagination of the intellect, lead her in many wandering ways. Tasting but few of the actual joys, the triumphs, and the trials of life, from the harem of her slavery her fancy has wandered with the winds. In her mind the unique and fatal experimenter, she has known all crimes, all horrors, as well as martyrdoms and joys. And this, while her gentle feminine hands have ministered to suffering, her voice has cheered, her smile has illumined, and her divine patience has endured.

Consider these lines — their spiritual intuition is the parallel of Wordsworth in his limpid moods; their knowledge, like a single glow of summer lightning, illumines all the darkened land as the glimmering patient light of Bourget's candle in cycles of encyclopedics will never do.

Behold the woman!

"*Beauté des femmes, leur faiblesse et ces mains pâles,
Qui font souvent le bien et peuvent tout le mal.*"

The appealing weakness of women is the first note, invariably stronger than command — and then the reference to their hands. This is very characteristic of Verlaine — they haunt him.

"*Les chères mains qui furent miennes,
Toutes petites, toutes belles.*"

. . . . . .

"*Mains en songes — main sur mon âme.*"

The last is a very poignant line — and again in "Ariettes Oubliées," —

"*Le piano que baise une main frêle.*"

Then comes the reflection as to the eyes of women, profoundly true and observant, contained in the last two verses of the first stanza: —

"*Et ces yeux où plus rien ne reste d'animal
Que juste assez pour dire 'assez' aux fureurs mâles!*"

Then the next stanza : —

"*Et toujours, maternelle endormeuse des râles,
Même quand elle ment —.*"

Here is the creature who could be both nurse and courtesan — concise and convincing classification.

Then he continues relating how, as man as well as poet, he has vibrated to the clear soprano of

"*Cette voix ! Matinal
Appel, ou chant bien doux à vêpres, ou frais signal,
Ou beau sanglot qui va mourir au pli des châles ! . . .*"

How he has dreamed over the tender sentiment of her twilight song, and been melted and conquered by the still greater, more beautiful appeal of the emotional soul for love and understanding, — "*beau sanglot*" indeed!

Then comes the wonderful third stanza, and its denunciation of man's brutality and selfishness.

"*Hommes durs ! Vie atroce et laide d'ici-bas !
Ah ! que du moins, loins des baisers et des combats,
Quelque chose demeure un peu sur la montagne.*"

Here is the appeal for sentiment, for the love of the spirit, choked in the throats of dumb and suffering women.

CHAP-BOOK ESSAYS

By Mrs. Reginald de Koven

" *Quelque chose du cœur,*" he repeats and persuades, "*enfantin et subtil.*"
" *Bonté, respect! car qu'est-ce qui nous accompagne,
Et vraiment, quand la mort viendra, que reste-t-il?*"

From him, the convict poet, from this heart rotten with all the sins of fancy and of deed, bursts this plea — as naive as it is earnest, for the spiritual in love — for sentiment, the essence of the soul. Strange anomaly — stranger still that it should be he who has understood.

Three lines more, from an early poem called "*Vœu,*" of such condensed significance and biting truth as lacks a parallel.

" *O la femme à l'amour câlin et rechauffant,
Douce, pensive et brune, et jamais étonnée,
Et qui parfois vous baise au front, comme un enfant.*"

What a portrait, typical and individual — "*jamais étonnée,*" my sisters, what an accusation!

. . . . . .

Verlaine is dead. The last shred of that ruined soul which has for years been rotting away in chance Parisian brasseries, has loosened its hold upon life and slipped into the unknown; but the poetry he has left behind him, with its sighs and bitter sobbings, and its few gleams of beauty and of joy, contains the essence of his strange nature.

Although repudiating the responsibility of the position, he was the founder and leader of that school of poetic expression which has most importantly distinguished the end of his century.

Half faun, half satyr, his nature was allied to baseness and brutal animalism, but possessed a strange and childish naïveté which remained with him to the last, and a spirit remotely intact in the chaos of his wayward senses, whence issued songs of matchless purity and inimitable music.

Degeneration
By
Alice Morse Earle

DEGENERATION

I WRITE this paper as a solemn, an earnest warning, an appeal to the unsuspecting and serene general public not to read Dr. Max Nordau's book "Degeneration." I give this word of admonition with much the same spirit of despairing yet powerless misery as might animate the warning of any slave to a despised habit, a hashish-eater, an opium smoker, an alcoholic inebriate. I have read this book of Dr. Nordau's, and through it I am become the unwilling victim of a most deplorable, most odious, most blighting habit, — that of searching for degenerates. I do not want or like to do this, but I do it instinctively, mechanically. The habit has poisoned all the social relations of my life, has entered into my views of the general public; it has sapped my delight in novelty, choked my admiration of genius, deadened my enthusiasm, silenced my opinions; and it has brought these wretched conditions not only into my regard of matters and persons of the present times, but retrospectively it

Degeneration

has tainted the glories of history. All this is exceeded by the introspective blight of the book through exacting a miserable and mortifying self-examination, which leads to the despairing, the unyielding conclusion that I am myself a degenerate.

The book is, unfortunately, so explicit in explanation as to lure every reader to amateur investigation. Indeed, such a vast array of mental and physical traits are enumerated as stigmata — the marks of the beast — as to paralyze the thoughtless, and to make the judicious grieve. Our mental traits we can ofttimes conceal from public view, our moral traits we always conceal, but many of our physical charcateristics cannot, alas, be wholly hidden. Dr. Nordau enumerates many physical stigmata, all interesting, but perhaps the most prominent, most visible one, is the degenerate malformation of the ear.

I was present recently, at an interesting function whereat the subject of the evening was discussion of this book "Degeneration." In the course of a brilliant and convincing address one of the lecturers chanced to name that most hateful and evident stigma, the ear-mark, so to speak, of the accursed. Though simple were his words, as subtle as sewer-gas was his poison; as all-pervading and penetrating as the sand-storm in the desert, it entered every brain in the room. I speedily and furtively glanced from side to side at my neighbors' ears, only to find them regarding mine with expressions varying from inquisitiveness through surprise and apprehension, to something closely approaching disgust. After the discussion was ended, friends advanced to speak with me; they shook hands, not looking with pleasant greeting into my eyes, but openly staring at my ears.

Now, that would be necessarily most abhorrent to every one, — to quote Spenser: —

"For fear lest we like rogues should be reputed
And for eare-marked beastes abroad be bruited."

And it is specially offensive to me — it would be anyway, for my ears are not handsome; but worse still must be admitted, they are not normal. They answer every purpose of hearing and of restraining my hat from slipping down over my eyes and on my neck, which is all I have demanded of them hitherto. But now I know that as emblems of my mental and moral characteristics they are wholly remiss, even degraded. They are .079 larger than normality;

Degeneration

they stand out from my head at an angle which exhibits 2° too much obtusity; the lobule displays .17 too little pendulosity; and, worst of all, the fossa scaphoida of my pinna is basely unconvoluted. I am sore ashamed of all this. I think of having the twin base betrayers of my degenerate nature shaved off in spots, and already I tie them close to my head at night in a feeble attempt at improvement. But I am not in my callow youth; I fear they have not been bent in the way they should be inclined, that their degeneracy is irremediable.

It is not through physical stigmata alone that I find myself branded. I find that I am impulsive, I have a predilection for inane reverie, and for search for the bases of phenomena — all sad traits. Worst of all, I have "the irresistible desire of the degenerate to accumulate useless trifles." Nordau says, "It is a stigmata of degeneration, and has had invented for it the name oniomania or buying craze. The oniomaniac is simply unable to pass by any lumber without feeling an impulse to acquire." When I read that sentence I glanced guiltily at my cabinets of old china — well, I could use it on the table and thus make it unstigmatic; at my Dutch silver — I might

CHAP-BOOK ESSAYS

By Alice Morse Earle

melt it up and sell it; my books, my autographs, my photographs, all may find some excuse; but how can I palliate my book-plates, or ever live down having gone for a year through every village, city, and town where I chanced or sought to wander, asking at every jeweller's, silversmith's, and watch-repairer's, "Have you any bridges of old verge watches?" I fear those watch-bridges stamp me an oniomaniac. And am I wholly free from Lombroso's graphomania? Have I not an insane desire to write? I conceal my obsession, but it ever influences me. I may confess also (since I confess at all) that I have rupophobia (fear of dirt), iophobia (fear of poison), nosophobia (fear of sickness), belenophobia (fear of needles — especially on the floor), and one or two other wretched obsessions, particularly an inordinate love for animals, upon which I had hitherto rather bridled as the mark of a tender nature.

But let me dwell no more on my own peculiar stigmata, but show how — to paraphrase Prior:

"All earth is by the ears together
Since first that horrid book come hither."

I haunt photograph shops, look over the frontis-

Degeneration

pieces of illustrated magazines, and various collections of likenesses, until I am wearied to the core of looking at the ears of prominent persons, and it brings forth a sense of profound, of heartfelt gratitude that Daguerre was not born till this century, almost till our own day, and that thus the ears of centuries of countless geniuses are disguised in their counterfeit presentments by the meaningless conventionalities of the artist's brush, which represent in peaceful and happy monotony and perfection that unfortunate, that abhorred member. I plainly see, too, what the result of all this will be. I picture to myself the poet of the future, hooded, veiled, to conceal his features; robed in flowing drapery to cover his feet; with his hands in a muff; living alone to hide his personal habits; studiously avoiding the subject of his health; painstaking in showing no decided preferences; void of passion lest he be deemed erotic; void of epigram or humor lest his wit be taken as earnest; until I sigh mournfully for the time spoken of in Genesis, when "there was no more earing."

I will not sign my name to this heartfelt communication, since it would have no weight as the cognomen of either a genius or a mattoid, and perhaps the cry of warning will be more heeded from a suffering incognito. Besides, I do not wish to be shunned by my fellow-creatures as one who is determined to know their innermost worst, with as cruel a mental insistence, and with a method genetic to that employed by the Inquisition in penetrating the brain of its victims by pouring boiling oil in the ears. Nor am I willing to have such an odious position in society that none of my friends will visit me, or come in my presence unless fortified with ear-muffs against my insinuating gaze.

The Pleasures of Historiography
By
Alice Morse Earle

THE PLEASURES OF HISTORIOGRAPHY

THE PLEASURES OF THE CHASE

I AM an historiographer; and being desirous and assiduous of accuracy in my statements, I am given to recourse to first sources of authority, to the fountain springs of great events; I am a scientifically historical Gradgrind; I build up my histories inductively from facts by the most approved scientific processes. And I can say with feeling and with emphasis, in the words of Sir Thomas Browne: " Sure, a great deal of conscience goes into the making of a history."

A few days ago the need of exact knowledge upon a certain point in the criminal history of the colonies determined me to seek my information in the most unerring and unimpeachable historical records we have, those of the Criminal Court. Those I sought were of a large city, I might say of Chicago, only she has no colonial records; so I frankly reveal that I wished to search the records of the criminal courts of New Amsterdam.

The Pleasures of Historiography

Now I had read a score of times, and heard a score of times more in the glibly-rounded sentences of elegant historical lectures, patriotic addresses, commemorative "papers" of patriotic-hereditary societies, that to the municipal honor of that very large frog in a puddle, viz. : New York, which grew out of the pollywog New Amsterdam, all records of colonial times of that city were still preserved, were cherished as sacred script in that fitting cabinet, the venerable Hall of Records in the City Hall Park. Thus introduced, I ventured to its gates.

It is an ancient, dingy building, whose opening portals thrust you upon a cage-like partition strongly suggestive of a menagerie, and also olfactorily suggestive of the menageries' accompaniment, "an ancient and a fish-like" — nay, more, a bird- and beast-like smell.

A doorway on either side of the cage lead to various desks and rooms, and enclosures and closets, all labelled with well-worn signs; and as I glanced bewildered from placard to placard, from sign to sign, there approached that blessed and gallant metropolitan engine for the succor of feminine ignorance, incapacity, and weakness — a policeman. Gladly did

By Alice Morse Earle

I follow in his sturdy wake to the office of the Clerk of Records, who would know all about it. Alas! he was out. A callow, inky youth, his deputy, had never heard of any Dutch records, and did n't believe there were any in New York. My policeman had vanished. The youth leaned out of his latticed window, pointed round a corner to an enclosed office: "Go ask *him*, he can tell you." I went and asked him; for a third time I told my tale, already rehearsed to policeman and youth. "I wish to see the colonial records of the criminal courts in New York in the seventeenth century. Part are in Dutch. I hear they have been translated, and that the English translation is here, for the use of the public. If this is not so, I wish to see the original Dutch and English records from the year 1650 to 1700."

It is impossible to overstate the expression of blank surprise and incredulity with which this inquiry was greeted. The official vouchsafed one curt answer: "I never heard of such a thing as a Dutch trial in the criminal courts of New York, and I don't believe there ever was one. If so, *he* will know."

"He" was a haven, for his office was labelled

Satisfaction — and he was satisfactory. After a fourth explanation of my desires, he answered me with the elaborately patient and compassionate politeness usually employed by men in business and public offices to a woman's apparently useless inquiries. He said gently : "Only deeds and transfers are here in the Hall of Records; those records you wish to see are all in the County Clerk's office, over there."

Over there was the court-house of Tweed's inglorious fame. Within the said office four transfers, from book-keeper to messenger, to civil clerk, to County Clerk, found me, after four more dogged repetitions, encaged myself in a dingy wire prison, surrounded by millions of compartments with papers and deeds, and flanked by scores of spittoons. Errand boys, messengers, aged porters, young attorneys, came and went, papers were given and received with mechanical rapidity and precision by the monarch of the cage, an elderly Irishman, smooth-shaven, massive-featured, inscrutable, blank of expression, who finally turned to me with civil indifference. But this was not the right place for me to come; those records were at the court-house at Ninth Street, where the criminal courts were held. I patiently prepared to assail the Ninth Street abode of Themis, not without an unworthy suspicion that this Hibernian Sphinx sent me there to get rid of me. But a gentleman-like and eavesdropping bystander proffered his advice: "Those records you want are in the office of the Clerk of the Court of Common Pleas, in the third story of this building." And he thrust me with speed in the ascending elevator. The room pointed out to me as my goal proved to be the Supreme Court, a scene of peaceful dignity, but, alas, there was no such officer anywhere as the Clerk of the Court of Common Pleas. Gloomily turning to the Surrogate's office to examine the will of this Dutch criminal whom I was running to earth, mine eyes encountered this sign: Office of the Court of Common Pleas. Certainly this was the office and the records were here, though the clerk was not. Other clerks there were; to the most urbane for the tenth time I told my tale, and finally was shown the records. "These are in Dutch," I said; "will you show me the English translation?" "Are they in Dutch?" he answered with some animation. "I never knew that. I have been here twenty years, and no one has ever asked to see them before."

The Pleasures of Historiography

Of course there was no English translation. I can read and translate printed Dutch with ease; but seventeenth century Dutch differs more from modern Dutch than does old French from the French of to-day. Add to this the unique variations in spelling of the Dutch clerks, the curious chirography, the faded ink, and no antiquary will be surprised to learn that an hour had passed ere I had read enough of those records to learn that they were wholly civil cases, boundary disputes, adjustment cases, etc. I wearily rose to leave, when a newly-arrived person of authority said airily: "I can tell you all about those old Criminal Court records. They are all over in the City Hall, in the office of the Superintendent of City Affairs." I trust I showed becoming credulity and gratitude.

I walked out into the beautiful little park, aglow with beds of radiant scarlet and yellow tulips, that remembered and significantly commemorated their Holland ancestors and the old Dutch-American town, even if the city's servants knew them not; and I strolled under the trees and breathed with delight the fresh air of heaven; for wherever men congregate in offices, there ventilation is as naught.

CHAP-BOOK ESSAYS

By Alice Morse Earle

I sought the Superintendent's office. To him, ignominiously but cheerfully ensconced in the cellar-like basement, I descended, where glimmered a light so dim, so humid, that I had a sense of being in subaqueous rather than subterranean depths, and I was struck with the civic humor that placed the Superintendent *subter omnia*.

He really knew nothing about these records, but there was a man in the Library who would know. Through underground tunnels and cemented passages and up a narrow staircase, I reached the noble above-ground abode of our municipal corporation.

Here all was radiant with prosperity. No lean and hungry race filled those corridors and chambers; jocund and ruddy were all, as were our city fathers of yore who drank vast tuns of sack-posset and ale. Well may we say when on those men and on these we gaze: Nobly wert thou named Manhattan! — *the place where all drank together!*

Mighty is Manhattan and great even the reflection of her power. Neither poverty-stricken nor meagre of flesh am I, but I shrank into humble insignificance before those well-fed aggrandizations of the city's glory and prosperity who bourgeoned through the corridors of our modern Stadt Huys; and I fain would have saluted them with respectful mien and words as of yore as " Most Worshipful, Most Prudent, and Very Discreet, their High Mightinesses," — not Burgomasters and Schepens, but Aldermen and Councilmen, — but the tame conventionalities of modern life kept me silent.

In the Library the sought-for man sent me to the Clerk of the Common Council, who in turn bade me be seated while he lured from an adjoining "closet," as old Pepys called his office, one who would be glad to tell me all about everything relating to those ancient days.

Here was something tangible. Glad to tell me! In truth he was. Never have I seen such a passion for talking. Forth poured a flood of elaborate Milesian eloquence, in which intricate suggestions, noble patriotic sentiments, ardent historical interest, warm sympathy in my researches, and unbounded satisfaction and glowing pride over New York's honorable preservation of the records of her ancestors all joined. Nevertheless and notwithstanding, when I ran my fat but sly and agile political fox to earth, and made him answer me directly, I simmered down merely this one solid fact: "If ye go to Mr. De Lancy's office in the Vanderbilt Building, he can tell ye where thim ricords is, an' no one ilse in this city can."

I tendered as floriated and declamatory a farewell expression of gratitude as my dull tongue could command to my city authority, who was, I am led to believe from the tablet on the office from which he emerged, a common councilman, but who might have been a score of glorious aldermen distilled and expressed and condensed into one, so rotund, so ruby-colored, so shining, so truly grand was he, so elegant, albeit loose, of attire, so glittering with gold and precious stones. As I thanked him in phrases sadly etiolated in comparison with his own glowing pauses, "Madam," said he, "are you satisfied, and may I ask your name and residence?" "You may," said I, "I came to study history, and I was sent to the Satisfaction Clerk, and I found satisfaction, though not in the wonted legal form." "But ye have n't told me yer name," said he. "I have not," said I; "good day."

The Bureau of Literary
   Revision
By
Alice Morse Earle

THE BUREAU OF LITERARY REVISION

OUR beloved friend Charles Lamb once wrote of his Essays of Elia : —

"One of these professors, on my complaining that these little sketches of mine were anything but methodical, and that I was unable to make them otherwise, kindly offered to instruct me on the method by which the young gentlemen in his seminary were taught to compose English themes."

When, with the solemn thoughts brought to each soul at the "turn of the year," we recount to ourselves our many mercies, let us never fail to remember with gratitude that the magnanimous offer of that seminary professor was never accepted.

We do not have to wait to-day for chance offers from solemn professors of instruction and revision in literary composition ; "the method by which young gentlemen in the seminary are taught to compose" is thrust upon us at every hand. "Bureaus of revision" and "Offices of literary criticism" abound and thrive and become opulent through examining, correcting, and revising the work of confiding authors.

The Bureau of Literary Revision

We are told with pride that in one bureau alone three thousand manuscripts a year were thus revised. Among those three thousand young fledglings of authors there may *not* have been a Charles Lamb, but the lamentable thought also will arise that there *may* have been a Charles Lamb, and that his unmethodical little "sketches" may have been pruned or amplified, or arranged and revised till they proved true "English themes."

There is a wearying monotony in the make-up of many of our periodicals, some of those even of large circulation. There is a lack of literary color, a precise and proper formation of each sentence, and a regularity of ensemble which is certainly grammatical but is fully as uninteresting as grammar. A surfeit of these exactly formal "English themes" has made the gasping public turn to some of our literary freaks and comets with a sensation as if seeking an inspiration of fresh air after mental smothering.

I attribute this too frequent monotony, and even stultification of composition, to the "literary reviser." — the trail of the serpent is over all our press.

And what does this literary revision offer for the large fees paid? One alleged benefit is the correction of punctuation. It certainly performs this service; but the editor and proofreader in any responsible publishing-house will, as a duty, correct with precision the punctuation of any paper or book printed by the house. A benefit alleged by one circular is "a pruning of too riotous imagination." I groaned aloud as I read this threat. Too riotous imagination to-day! when we long for imagination and long in vain; when a wooden realism thrusts its angular outlines in our faces from every printed page. "To curb the use of adjectives" is another of the reviser's duties. The meagre style too often seen of late may arise from this curbing.

The most astonishing aspect of this bureau of revision is shown in the patience with which authors endure its devastations. They confidingly send into this machine the tenderly nourished children of their brains, dressed with natural affection in all the frills and ruffles of rhetoric, and receive them home again with ornaments torn away, laid in a strait-jacket which has been cut with rigid uniformity, and made with mathematical precision — and yet they kiss the rod that turned the natural children of their brains into wretched little automatons.

The Bureau of Literary Revision

I would not judge all revision bureaus by one; but I must give my experience at the hands of a very reputable one. I had written four books of more than average sale, and had been ever commended by the press for my grammatical construction, when I sent to a bureau for criticism a short magazine-paper. It was returned to me full of very large and legible corrections — or rather alterations such as these: Where I wrote of my heroine being *dressed in*, etc., my reviser placed *gowned in;* where I wrote *the little child*, the reviser altered to *the young babe;* where I said *nothing happened after this*, to my horror, in heroic blue-pencilled letters, I read my pet aversion, *nothing transpired.* Where a compound sentence contained several clauses with verbs in the past tense, all dependent clauses were made participial in form; not always to the advantage in elegance, never of moment or indeed of real difference in grammatical construction.

I must confess that I did not send to this bureau my real name, as palpably too well known to men of literary ilk. My three dollars' worth of advice was contained in a single sentence: "Your style is fair, but commonplace; if you practise literary composition you may succeed; but this article is, in our judgment, not salable."

I had the pleasure of sending the paper immediately to a well-known magazine and receiving therefrom in payment a check for fifty dollars.

Mr. Meredith and his Aminta

By
Lewis E Gates

MR. MEREDITH AND HIS AMINTA

IN his latest book the choppiness of Mr. Meredith's style and the restless tacking of his method are as great as ever, and those worthy people who delight in the smooth seas and the steady zephyrs of ordinary English fiction will find their experience of "Lord Ormont and his Aminta" very much of a stormy channel-passage. But to people with sound nerves and adventurous spirits the experience is sure to be bracing and exhilarating. Perhaps the most surprising single effect that you get from "Lord Ormont" is that of the tingling vitality of the author. You can hardly realize while reading the book that you have to do with a writer who has been for forty years a tireless worker in literature, and who published his first venture in fiction two years before George Eliot's first story. The style in "Lord Ormont" has all the audacity of a first rebellion against tradition and convention; the sentences rush forward in all possible rhythms except the languorous ones of the dilettante or the "faultily faultless" ones of the precisian or pedant; the imagination is restlessly self-assertive in its embodiment of every abstract idea in an image for eye or for ear; the tone is almost boisterous in its hilarity or brusqueness; and finally the book sounds everywhere the note of the future, and prophesies change and new social conditions without a touch of misgiving or regret. Perhaps in no earlier work has Mr. Meredith been so aggressive and, at the same time, so confident and buoyant.

As for Mr. Meredith's technique, it remains in the new book substantially what it has always been, and many of the general effects he produces are familiar to his admirers and delightful in their recurrence. Where save in Mr. Meredith's fiction can there be found such brilliance of surface? such vividness of dramatic portrayal? Or at any rate where is vividness so reconciled with suggestiveness of interpretation? concrete beauty with abstract truth? In all his novels he sends our imaginations flashing over the surface of some portion of life; he calls up before us this portion of life in all its fine contrasts of color and form, of storm and sunshine, of mid-day and moonlight; and yet at the same time he constrains us to pierce below the surface and to understand intuitively why the drama moves this way or that, what forces are in conflict, what passions are flushing or blanching the cheek, what fancies or ideals are making the eyes dream on a distant goal.

More nearly than any other living novelist, Mr. Meredith succeeds in overcoming the difficulties forced on the writer of fiction by the double appeal of life. Life is a pageant and life is a problem; it smites on the senses and allures the imagination, but it also challenges the intellect; it has power and beauty, but it has also significance. Now most writers of fiction who reveal to us the inner meaning of life allow its beauty and power to fade into shadowy vagueness; and those who give us the dramatic value of life too often lack penetration and philosophic insight. One of Mr. Meredith's greatest claims to distinction lies in the fact that he, better than any other English novelist, has reconciled this conflict between vividness of portrayal and depth of interpretation. He has grasped English life in all its enormous range and mass and complexity; he has flashed it before us in all its splendid vividness for eye and ear and imagination; and at the same time he has made it suggestive to thought, has comprehended it through and through in its subtlest relations, and in portraying it has breathed into it the breath of a philosophical spirit.

If we analyze Mr. Meredith's pages carefully, we find very few of those long disquisitions on character with which the pages of a pyschological novelist are covered. He deals almost as constantly with acts, with dialogue, with what meets the senses, the eye and the ear, as the elder Dumas. It is a mimic world of images he gives, not a globe of the earth with scientific terms and black marks on yellow pasteboard. He is always primarily an artist, not a psychologist or a descriptive sociologist. Too often when we finish one of George Eliot's stories we feel that she has explained her characters so exhaustively that we should not know them if we met them on the street. We have had so much to do with their ganglia and their nervous systems, and with the ashes of their ancestors, that we have little notion of the characters as actual living people. If a psychological novelist were to write out a professional analysis of one's best friend, it may fairly be doubted whether one would recognize the description. In fact, in real life it is only criminals whom we are expected to recognize by anthropometric memoranda, — by the length of the index finger, the breadth of the ear, the distance between the eyes, and by the lines on the finger-tips.

Now Mr. Meredith avoids all anthropometric statistics and chemical analysis, and gives us the very counterfeit presentment of men and women as in actual life they go visibly and audibly past us; and yet he so seizes his moments for portraiture that the soul, the inner life, the character, photographs itself on the retina of a sensitive on-looker like a composite picture. He makes all his characters and scenes, and all the life he portrays, instinct with truth; and yet this truth is implicit; the author very rarely indulges in pretentious talk on these topics. For the most part, he is apparently busy putting before us the picturesque aspects of life and its dramatic moments.

This fondness of his for brilliance of surface, for vividness of portrayal, accounts for many peculiarities of Mr. Meredith's method, — among them for the use of what may be termed *Meredith mosaic*.

His opening chapters are nearly always curious composites, made up of dozens of little speeches, little acts, little scenes, collected from a series of years, and fitted together into a more or less homogeneous whole. He dislikes formal exposition; he instinctively shrinks from discoursing through wearisome pages on the early lives of the actors in his story, on the formative influences, for example, which had moulded the characters of Aminta and Weyburn up to the moment when the continuous action of "Lord Ormont" begins. Yet the "fuller portraiture" requires that this knowledge be in some way ensured to his readers. Hence he puts before us such skilfully chosen bits of Aminta's and Weyburn's early lives, that while our imaginations are always kept busy with words and tones and acts and looks, we are at the same time inveigled into a knowledge of minds and hearts and motives. Chapters constructed on this plan are curiously without continuity of action, and often seem puzzling in their fragmentariness. But they combine, in an unusual degree, vividness of portrayal with suggestiveness of interpretation.

Another means by which Mr. Meredith secures

his brilliance of surface, his glowing color, is through his lavish use of figures. Mr. Meredith is a poet subdued by the spirit of his age to work in its most popular form, the novel; but even in prose his imagination will not be gainsaid, and everywhere we find in his style the sensuous concreteness and symbolism of poetry. "Absent or present, she was round him like the hills of a valley. She was round his thoughts — caged them; however high, however far they flew, they were conscious of her."
. . . "Aminta drove her questioning heart as a vessel across blank circles of sea where there was nothing save the solitary heart for answer." In no other contemporary English fiction do we come upon passages like these, and realize with a sudden pang of delight that we are in the region of poetry where imaginative beauty is an end in itself.

Very often, of old, it was Nature that enticed Mr. Meredith into these ravishing escapades; in "Lord Ormont" he seems pretty nearly to have broken with Nature. Yet, now and then, he puts before us a bit of the outside world with a compression of phrase, a brilliance of technique, and an imaginative atmosphere, not easily to be matched.

"A wind was rising. The trees gave their swish of leaves, the river darkened the patch of wrinkles, the bordering flags amid the reed-blades dipped and streamed. . . .

"The trees were bending, the water hissing, the grasses all this way and that, like the hands of a delirious people in surges of wreck. . . .

"Thames played round them on his pastoral pipes. Bee-note and woodside blackbird, and meadow cow, and the leap of the fish of the silver rolling rings, composed the music."

But often as Mr. Meredith's imagination seeks and realizes the beautiful, it still more often works in the grotesque, and decks out his subject with arabesque detail. His satirical comment on the life he portrays finds its way to the reader through the constant innuendoes of figurative language.

"She probably regarded the wedding by law as the end a woman has to aim at, and is annihilated by hitting; one flash of success and then extinction, like a boy's cracker on the pavement. . . .

"Thither he walked, a few minutes after noon, prepared for cattishness. . . . He would have to crush her if she humped and spat, and he hoped to be allowed to do it gently. . . . Lady Charlotte put on her hump of the feline defensive; then his batteries opened fire and hers barked back on him."

That Mr. Meredith often overworks these grotesque figures even his warmest admirers must admit. There is a passage in the opening chapter of "Beauchamp's Career," where for two pages he describes the creation of an artificial war-panic under the figure of "a deliberate saddling of our ancient nightmare of Invasion." Before Mr. Meredith consents to have done with this figure, even his most obsequious admirers must be desolated at his persistence. One is tempted to borrow the figure, and to call this kind of writing Mr. Meredith's nightmare style, when a figure like a nightmare gets the bit in its teeth and goes racing across country with the author madly grimacing on its back.

In point of fact, the imaginative or figurative quality of his style is probably what costs Mr. Meredith most readers. His perpetually shifting brilliances prove very wearisome to certain eyes. He is too much of a flash-light, or has too much of the flourish of a Roman candle, for those who pride themselves on their devotion to the steady effulgence of the petroleum evening-lamp. Hazlitt used to tell people who objected to Spenser's "Faery Queen" on the ground of the allegory, that, after all, the poetry was good poetry and the allegory would not bite them. But if you similarly urge upon the objectors to Mr. Meredith's style, that a story of his is too great to be neglected because of mere questions of phrasing, they are very likely to tell you that they cannot see the story for the glare of the style; just there lies their point.

Undoubtedly, at times, Mr. Meredith seems glaringly wilful in his rejection of ordinary rhetorical canons; there is something, too, of a flourish in his eccentricity; and often, apparently out of sheer bravado, he inserts in his stories rollickingly grotesque passages, or throws at the critics long sentences full of the clash of metaphors. One may fancy his exclaiming with Browning, —

"Well, British public, ye that like me not,
(God love you!) and will have your proper laugh
At the dark question, laugh it! I laugh first."

But after all, isn't he right in maintaining his individuality against all-comers? Can any one who understands the true nature of an individual style and its self-revealing power, wish Mr. Meredith's style less racy, less figurative, less original? Surely, words and phrases that bear the impress of a nature like Mr. Meredith's are better worth while than those that have become smooth and shiny with conventional use, — always providing that the metal be twenty-carats fine. The intimacy of the relation that Mr. Meredith's style makes possible between ordinary folk and a great and original personality is something that cannot be too highly prized in these days of conventionality and democratic averages. The words of most writers now-a-days give us no clew to their individualities. "Tête-à-tête with Lady Duberly?" exclaims the man in the play. "Nay, sir, tête-à-tête with ten-thousand people." Private ownership in words and phrases seems in danger of becoming, even more speedily than private ownership in land, a thing of the past. The distinction of Mr. Meredith's style is something to be devoutly grateful for. One would infinitely rather have a notion of the world as it gives an account of itself in Mr. Meredith's mind, than a conventional scheme of things drawn out in the stereotyped phrases of the rhetorician.

Possibly, however, there is one sound reason for wishing that Mr. Meredith would be just a little less insistent on differences, and would now and then "mitigate the rancor of his tongue;" that reason is based on the fear that in this stupid world of ours compromise and conventionality are needed to secure any adequate hearing. It seems a great pity that so many people should be frightened away from Mr. Meredith's work by its mannerism, and should be oblivious to some of the most suggestive current criticism of modern life. To Americans it seems specially to be regretted that English people should be so little receptive of the ideas of the most comprehensive and the least insular of their novelists. Mr. Meredith has grasped English life in its whole range and in all its vast complexity. He has dealt with the high and the low, with rustic and cockney, with plebeian and aristocrat, with the world of letters and the world of art and the world of fashion, with the modern "conquerors" of social power and position, and with the hereditarily great. All this vast range of life he has portrayed with equal vividness and with the same unfailing sympathy and insight; and yet his point of view is always curiously

By Lewis E. Gates

beyond the radius of the British Isles, and many of his implications are by no means favorable to the present organization of English social and political life. Of course, it may be this very lack of insularity that prevents a better understanding between him and his public. Detachment on his part may make attachment on their part impossible. And yet this ought not to be so ; for despite his occasional severities and the all-pervading independence and individuality of his tone, no one has loved English life more heartily, studied it more painstakingly, or represented it more patriotically. Indeed, certain of its important aspects can be found adequately portrayed only in Mr. Meredith's pages ; for example, the genuine irresponsibleness of the most brilliant English life. No other novels offer us such pictures of the world of the luxuriously idle and systematically frivolous, of the habits and homes of the people who have never been wont to give an account of themselves to others, who have made idling into a fine art, and feel that the land exists for them to shoot over, and the sea for them to sail on in yachts. The so-called society-novelist succeeds admirably with the gowns and the etiquette of this region, but gives us for its inhabitants a lamentable lot of insipidities. But Mr. Meredith's aristocrats have brains as well as deportment and decorations; they have the mental and moral idiom, the wit and the culture and the weight of men of birth and position, their prejudices, too, and perversities. That some wildness and even rankness of style should keep the British public from enjoying Mr. Meredith's vigorous and sympathetic studies of its idolized "upper classes" seems strange; and even more regrettable than strange it seems to those who find running all through Mr. Meredith's patriotic portrayal subtle insinuations of a criticism of English life most uninsular in its tenor and most salutary in its drift.

As to the precise value of the lesson latent in "Lord Ormont," there is, of course, much dubious questioning possible. The points at issue, however, are of a kind on which perhaps only the Ulysses of the matrimonial ocean, "much-experienced men" in the storms and sunshine of married life, are in a condition to pronounce. Nevertheless ordinary people may at least admire the conscientious care with which Mr. Meredith has safeguarded his dangerous advice and his somewhat revolutionary plea for the freedom of woman. His preceding novel, "One of our Conquerors," was from first to last a strenuously faithful study of the penalties that follow infringement of social conventions in the matter of marriage. The book might have been named "Mrs. Burman's Revenge." Mrs. Burman concentrated in her unprepossessing person all the mighty forces of prejudice which the society of the western world puts into play to protect one of its sacred institutions, marriage. Poor Nataly, who had ventured after happiness outside of conventional limits, lost happiness and finally life itself solely through her agonizingly persistent consciousness of her false adjustment to her social environment. She had built her house below the level of the dikes, to use Weyburn's metaphor, and the ever-present danger wore upon her and sapped her life.

Having thus set forth with the elaborateness of a three-volume novel, and with the utmost power of his imagination, the almost resistless might of social conventions, their importance, and the danger of defying them, Mr. Meredith in his last book ventures to plead for the individual against society, and to assert the right of the individual occasionally to rebel against a blindly tyrannizing convention. "Laws are necessary instruments of the majority; but when they grind the sane human being to dust for their maintenance, their enthronement is the rule of the savage's old deity, sniffing blood-sacrifice."

The case of immolation that Mr. Meredith studies is meant, despite some very special features, to be typical. The veteran Lord Ormont stands as the representative, the most polished and prepossessing representative possible, of the class of men for whom woman is still merely the daintiest, the most exquisite toy that a benevolent Providence has created for the delectation of the sons of Adam. Weyburn is the ideal modern man of "spiritual valiancy," every whit as vigorous and virile as Lord Ormont, but mentally and morally of immeasurably greater flexibility, and keenly alive to the needs of his time and the signs of social change. He, too, is doubtless meant to be a type, — so far as Mr. Meredith allows himself in character-drawing the somewhat dangerous luxury of types; he is to be taken as the most efficient possible member of a modern social organization, where the standards of individual excellence are fixed, not primarily by the organism's need of defence against external foes, but by what is requisite for the inner expansion and peaceful evolution of society. Aminta, "the most beautiful woman of her time," has been half-secretly married to Lord Ormont in the Spanish legation at Madrid, after a few weeks of travelling courtship; forthwith she has become in his eyes *his* Aminta, his lovely Xarifa, his beautiful slave, whom his soul delighteth to honor, — with ever a due sense of the make-believe character of her sovereignty and with a changelessly cynical conviction of the essential inferiority of the feminine nature. From his "knightly amatory" adulation, from the caressing glances of his "old-world eye upon women," from his "massive selfishness and icy inaccessibility to emotion," Aminta finally revolts, and takes refuge with Weyburn because with him she finds "comprehension," "encouragement," "life and air," freedom to "use her qualities." "His need and her need rushed together somewhere down the skies."

Doubtless, all this seems dangerously near the old doctrine of elective affinities, on which organized society has never looked kindly. But once more we cannot but admire the care with which Mr. Meredith has limited his acceptance and recommendation of the principle. If it is to be operative only in a society in which a schoolmaster of spiritual valiancy is the popular hero, the ideal of manhood, and in which the most beautiful women of their time desert famous military leaders to become part-owners in boarding-schools, Mr. Meredith can hardly be accused of recommending very serious or far-reaching changes in the present state of the marriage contract.

Whatever one may think of the special moral of the book, the nobly optimistic tone of the whole is inspiriting. Mr. Meredith's vigorous optimism and his suggestion of endless vistas of social progress contrast curiously with Mr. Hardy's harping on the age of the earth, Druidical ruins, and the irony of a cruel Nature. Mr. Meredith, like his own Weyburn, is "one of the lovers of life, beautiful to behold, when we spy into them; generally their aspect is an enlivenment, whatever may be the carving of their features," or, we may add, the eccentricity of their style. He is one of those who "have a cold morning on their foreheads," and whose "gaze is to the front in hungry animation." His optimism is doubly grateful because it is not the optimism of untempered youth, but, like Browning's, the optimism of a man who has sounded and tried life in all its shallows and depths, has sailed far and wide over its surface, and yet possesses a genuine Ulysses-like hunger for achievement and belief in its worth. In this age when the decadents like the Philistines be upon us, and when the weariness of much learning and of much feeling weighs down so many eyelids, it seems strange that the virility and vigor and courage of Mr. Meredith do not find welcome everywhere among the sane-minded.

The Popularity of Poetry
By
Edmund Gosse

THE POPULARITY OF POETRY.

IS the commercial standard of literary success to be extended to poetry? This is a question that is raised by the peculiar conditions which have developed during the last two years, and it is one which it is important to attempt to solve. If poetry is to be judged by the extent to which it is sold, and especially in relation to the sales of prose fiction, then it must be admitted at once to be in a very sad quandary indeed. If, on the other hand, the status of poetry is to be discovered by a consideration of the degree to which it is talked about and written about, then no branch of contemporary literature would seem to be more flourishing. It is desirable to attempt to define what literary popularity is, and then to see how far the poets of to-day enjoy a share of it.

In its original meaning "popularity" signifies a courting of the popular favor; it is only in its modern and secondary use that the word takes the sense of a gaining of that good-will. Our old writers employed the word with a certain flavor of obsequiousness hanging about it. Among the Elizabethans to be "popular" was to have resigned something of the dignity of independent judgment. We have lost all that in these democratic days, and he is held the most honorable man who has contrived to please the largest number of individual voters, and that book the most successful which has appealed to the largest number of readers. Yet, even with us, literary popularity has not quite come to be synonymous with largeness of sales. We are not so mechanically statistical, even in the matter of our novels, and there are writers whose works sell in vast masses, who enjoy a kind of blind, contemptuous success, and who yet are scarcely to be called "popular." There are writers, too, of comic or sentimental verse, who are never mentioned among the poets, whose sales, nevertheless, by far exceed those of Mr. Swinburne. I remember how once, in the sacred Lodge of Trinity, and to the face of its fastidious master, the late Lord Houghton contended that the most prominent living poet of England was the writer of a song called "The Old Obadiah and the Young Obadiah."

At the moment when this whimsical theory was put forth, England possessed a poet of unsurpassed popularity. The case of Tennyson was a singular and, for future generations, a disturbing one. As we look down the history of our country, we may be surprised to see how few of our greatest bards have enjoyed wide popular favor in their life-time. Neither Shakespeare nor Milton, neither Wordsworth nor Coleridge, neither Shelley nor Keats, had any experience of general public acceptance. Dryden and Ben Jonson were illustrious, — they were scarcely popular. Among our really ambitious writers in verse, Cowley and Pope, Burns and Byron, and in his latest years Robert Browning, have alone enjoyed great popularity at all approaching that of Tennyson; and of these Burns is the most remarkable in this respect. Tennyson and Burns, a couple strangely assorted, — these are the two great names in poetry which have achieved, by purely poetic qualities, a lasting approbation from the people of Great Britain.

In the case of Burns, as in that of Béranger in France, the charm of the pure, natural lyric, uttered in the quintessence of its naïveté may be allowed to account for much of the popular acceptation. The universality of Tennyson is a more difficult problem, and one on which criticism has expended much speculation. The main thing at this moment is to admit and to note that popularity, and to see whether it is likely to be continued to later writers. In the first place, it is highly important to recognize that in the history of our poetry, now extending over at least six centuries, it has by no means been the rule that what was ultimately to be found incomparable received any special attention at the time of its production. Some poets have been mildly admired for a portion of their writings which we now regret that they should have produced, and have not been admired at all for their masterpieces. There is evidence to show that the exquisite lyrics of Herrick were not valued during his lifetime for any of the qualities which we now universally discern in them. Moore was greatly preferred to Shelley, not merely until the death of Shelley, but until long after the death of Moore. Much poetry becomes good, because public taste develops in the direction in which it was written; still more ceases to please, because the order of its thoughts and images is no longer in fashion. Criticism likes to conceive that its dicta are final, and talks familiarly about "immortality."

By Edmund Gosse

But, as a matter of fact, there are certain even of the old masters who are still on their probation, and a great social crisis might dethrone half Parnassus.

The death of Tennyson, following so closely on those of Browning and Matthew Arnold, produced a violent and disturbing crisis in our poetical history. At the first moment, in the agitation caused by the disappearance of these extremely dignified figures, and particularly by the extinction of Tennyson, the critics rashly asserted that poetry had ceased to develop; that it would henceforward be the pastime of children; and that it could no longer form a vital branch of our literature. Almost immediately it was perceived that whatever might happen, a neglect of verse was not imminent. We had long served under a gerantocracy, a tyranny by very old men. These venerable figures once removed, attention became fixed on men of the youngest generation. When all the ancient trees have fallen in the forest, the sturdiest saplings have room to expand. Of these some may be oaks and some may be alders, but all have a chance at last. We have seen no visible increase of public interest in the poets who already held high second or third rank (although the extreme respect with which the announcement of Christina Rossetti's death was received points to an understratum of appreciation for these), but we have certainly seen a sudden access of reputation among writers between thirty-five and twenty-five years of age. The pendulum of taste is ever swinging, and from the opinion that no one under eighty was worth reading, we have come to regard no one over thirty as deserving our attention.

It will be unfortunate, I think, if the poets allow themselves to be disturbed by the conditions of crisis through which we are now passing. I deprecate the use of phrases such as hail one or two young versemen as: "Swans emerging from the ruck of geese." A swan may once have been an ugly duckling; he has never been a goose, and exaggerations of this kind tend to encourage what is by far the most dangerous tendency of the literature of to-day, its commercial greediness. Coleridge, in his old age, told a friend of mine, who was then young, that he had never been one shilling the better off for all the verse he had ever printed. Mr. Dykes Campbell will tell us that this was an error of memory, but practically speaking it was true. In our own century, surrounded by admirers, living long past maturity, here was one of the truest poets of England confessing that poetry had been not so much a failure to him as a bankruptcy. Browning, to the very end of his days, through the period of his splendid late celebrity, could never have lived, however modestly, on what his poetry put into his pocket. These are the instances which the poet should bear in mind, nor allow himself to be dazzled by the almost inexplicable and entirely exceptional success of the career of Tennyson.

We are told that this is not a poetical age, nor ours a poetical country. No country and no age is poetical. If England is badly off, I have yet to learn that France or America, Italy or Germany, is in a more fortunate condition. In one of these countries, in Italy, as in England, it is true that attention is concentrated on certain young men of the latest generation. It is in Italy only, I think, that our youngest poets meet with rivals of their own value. Gabriele d'Annunzio and Rudyard Kipling are probably the most gifted persons under the age of thirty now writing verses in any part of the world. The Italians loudly praise the author of "Elegie

Romane," but if they buy his volumes to any appreciable extent, I am greatly misinformed. He is what Carducci and Panzacchi were before him, distinguished and illustrious, but not successful as the "female fictionist" understands success. No Italian poet, I think, in this day of the revival of Italian poetry, makes what could be called an appreciable income by his verse.

It would be indecorous to push the inquiry so far as to speculate how the increased interest in verse affects the pockets of our own younger poets. One hopes that they are fed with the flour of returns as well as with the honey of renown. But one doubts whether their pretty "limited editions," their choruses of praise, their various celebrity, are symptoms of more than a very moderate popularity. They would think it unkind if one were to say that one wished them no more pudding than their great forefathers enjoyed. In point of fact, one wishes for every true artist the maximum of practical appreciation of his art. But if they break their hearts because they are not Tennyson, they will be silly fellows. A poet need feel no sense of failure because his books do not lie on every parlor-table in Brompton, or because no movement is made towards his being called up into the House of Lords. Success in poetry has not been, and we may hope that it never will be, a matter in which income-tax collectors can take an interest.

More, perhaps, than any other species of literature, poetry ought to be its own exceeding great reward. The verseman should write his verse with no other thought in his mind than that of relieving his heart of metrical pangs too acutely delicious to be borne. The verse being written, and then printed, the poet has done his work. He ought to have no further solicitude. He has adventured in a kind of writing in which less than in any other the element of ephemeral interest exists. If his stanzas are of true excellence, they will be as much admired in 1945 as in 1895, and perhaps more so. The best poetry does not grow old-fashioned. The poet should consider that he is not engaged in the timid coasting-trade of the novelist; he has put out on the vast seas, and if the risks of sinking are great, there is the chance of reaching the Golden Isles. He works, we will not say for immortality, since that is a vague and uncertain phrase, but for the future, and he ought to be content to miss the more facile successes of the immediate present. Poetry, after all, is not a democratic art. It appeals to the few, it "makes great music," as Keats puts it, "for a little clan," and it can by no means be sure, in the wild hurly-burly of our life, immediately to win the attention of those elect ears. But good verse, once printed, is never lost; sooner or later it is discovered, and fixed, like a jewel, into its proper drawer in the cabinet of the ages. To last forever, as a specimen, by the side of Lovelace or of Wolfe, should be better worth working for than to earn five thousand pounds as the author of a deciduous novel about the "New Woman." At all events, the poet had better try to think so, for the financial prosperity can by no possible chance be his.

Concerning Me and the
 Metropolis
By
Louise Imogen Guiney

CONCERNING ME AND THE METROPOLIS.

IT is my wish to make a confession, an extraordinary one for an American, to wit: I am no lover of Paris. This is putting it mildly. I had never misery elsewhere of which I could not get, and hold, the upper hand. Now we were there under pleasantest conditions, at good headquarters, within reach of things I profess to love: the crowd, the studios, the concerts and cafés, the lights of the Place de la Concorde, the parks, the Louvre, the river-boats, the circuses, the old schools, the National Library. We had sweet weather; we had health, youth, leisure; we had a menu; O shade of Angry Cat! (which, you must know, is French for the best of kings, Henry of Navarre) what a menu we did have! But over me and my hitherto unperturbed jollity there fell a deadly melancholy. My family shopped and sported, while I stood amid a thousand wheels in the Carrefour Montmartre, or in the lee of Molière's fountained house-wall, with tears bursting down these indignant and constitutionally arid cheeks. All day I wandered about alone, like a lunatic or a lover; by night I slept little, and had visions weird and gory. This lasted an entire autumn, which I count as lost out of my life, and during which I never once could lay salt on the tail of what had been myself. Something in that nervous latitude knocked out my congenital stoicism; I began to have all manner of unmanageable emotions, like an eighteenth-century heroine with the spleen or the vapors; I was more sentient, more intelligent, more humanistic, more capable of vast virtues and vices than would have seemed credible to the New England which bred me upon her sacred bean. A violent quarrelsomeness possessed me; whatever I saw and heard was an irritation; I believe I could have offered, in all soberness, to reform the Comédie Française, to unbuild the Tour Saint-Jacques, and to fight the Immortals, man by man. The bearing and gesture of the polite wee police were odious in my eyes, and the parlous Parisian nurslings appeared insufferably like goblins. Frequently, I would fall literally on the neck of that dear little bronze Faun tiptoeing at the entrance to the Gardens of the Luxembourg, on the side of the Boule-Miche, scolding him fiercely for being able to live and smile and dance in fatal Paris!

And the unwonted behavior of me, the upside-downing and inside-outing of whatever I had fondly supposed to be my "ways"! It is to be desired, in general, that I were a less unspiritual creature; but there, at least, I haunted the great churches, especially Saint-Sulpice, with its solemn evensong borne on six hundred voices of seminarian men and boys. Whereas I had ever the relish of a genuine antiquary for tombs and epitaphs, I bolted incontinently from the beaded wreaths of Père-la-Chaise, and paid with a fit of shuddering for my propinquity to historic ashes in Saint-Denis. It would confound any of my acquaintances to be told that I was a misanthrope or a royalist; yet I used to look after the ominous, noisy, big-hatted, blue-chinned, whip-cracking cabbies, and grind my teeth at them as at the whole incarnate Revolution, which they instantly bring to mind. As for the Louvre, it gave me no comfort; I crossed its threshold but seldom, for it tore me in pieces with the unbearable glory on its walls.

In fine, Paris had about driven me mad. While I strolled the Quarter, I had for company, step for step, now Abelard, now Jacques de Molay and his Templars, now the Maid, now Coligny or Guise, now the Girondists and André Chénier: the long procession of the wronging and the wronged, the disillusioned, the slain, which belongs to those altered and brightened streets. Strange theories inhabited me; I was no crass optimist any more. My head hummed with the tragic warning of Bossuet, which Persius uttered before him, that at the bottom of every knowable thing was nothingness. And all this with a bun in one fist, and in the other a gem of a duodecimo, bought at the quays for three sous, with a cloudless sky above, and every incentive, including poverty, towards fullest content and exhilaration.

In London I had been happy, and "clad in complete steel" against such alien moods as these. And to London, eventually, I had to go back, although M. S., who lives for art and Chicago, and who always knows what's what, compared me to a spook with no stomach for Paradise, whimpering for Hades and the sooty company thereof. But in London I was calm, normal, free, as by some eternal paradox.

One door in Paris I regretted to leave, for I went almost daily, like Little Billee and his cheerful colleagues, to the Morgue. I should have become a great novelist, had I taken my chances there a bit longer! Next to the Morgue, I was loath to part with the bridges, over which goes so much laughing and shining life, under which so much mystery is forever being fished up by aid of the torch and the prong. Ah, those men and women, stung, from the beginning, by the scorpions in that smooth, clean, treacherous air, and asking of the Seine water that it should quench immaterial fires!

So long as I have an eye to my own longevity and peace, I shall never put foot in Paris. Moreover, the place is painful, as having shaken to the base my smug opinion of myself. It taught me my moral ticklishness, and shrunk me into less than a cosmopolite; though I make puns again, I do so humbly, and out of a psychic experience. Nor must the item go unrecorded that I had a French ancestor, an unimportant personage remembered not then so much as since. He was born on the borders of Provence;

what Paris was to him, or whether he ever beheld it, I know not. It is possible that he may have burned his fingers there, and that his bullying spirit imposed upon mine this fantastic attraction of repulsion, this irrational hatred of what I knew all the time to be the most animated, the most consistent, and the most beautiful city in the world.

"Trilby"
By
Louise Imogen Guiney

"TRILBY" is two things. It is a little, simple, light-hearted story, lop-sided, discursive, having breaks and patches; and it is also already a masterpiece *hors concours,* so that when you come before it, the only sage remark you can make is dumb-show: that is, you may with great propriety take off your hat. Its background is so treated that it takes rank as a new thing in English fiction. Others since Mürger have attempted to draw the life of the Quarter, but none with this blitheness and winning charm, not even Mr. Henry Harland (Sidney Luska) in his idyllic "Land of Love," which deserves to be better known. The spirit of "Trilby" is the very essence of the best old English humor, as if Fielding, Steele, and Thackeray had collaborated upon it in Paradise (forgetting just a little the rules of their mundane grammar, the conditions of their mundane style!) and transfused into it their robust manly gayety and their understanding tenderness of

"Trilby"

heart. Indeed, its every page seems to breathe forth Thackeray's darling axiom: "Fun is good; Truth is better; Love is best of all." It is a capital illustration of the capital French thesis that a subject counts for nothing, but that the treatment of a subject counts for everything. Let the average readeress, a person of conventions, go through "Trilby" from cover to cover. Her attitude at the end is Mrs. Bagot's own: affectionate and bewildered surrender. "Trilby" itself is what its heroine ingenuously calls the "altogether." It is an elemental human book, staged without costumes, attractive for no spurious attribute, but only through its gentleness and candor. It constrains talk, only because it has so strengthened feeling.

As for the tone of it, it has escaped mysticism, by great good fortune. Hypnotism, apprehended and faintly feared from the first, is used with an exquisitely abstinent touch. There is nowhere too much of it, and therefore it becomes credible and tragic. Svengali's evil influence hangs over the victim whom it glorifies, like a premonition of the Greeks, formless, having no precisely indicated end or beginning. His soul passes; and the music in her forsakes her on the instant, and passes with him. You are not told this; you gather it. The tale is crowded with these inferences, and the dullest or cleverest reader is alike flattered at finding them. So with the relationship of Little Billee and his stricken Trilby, fading away among the cheery and loyal painters who take pleasure yet in her perfections : there is not, in the written record, so much as a private look or sigh between the two any more; only Trilby's saddened confession to a third person that her girlish bosom had subdued itself at last to a meek, motherly yearning over her wild little worshipper, who nearly won her at the nineteenth asking.

The final chapters are out of proportion ; chance, or weariness, led the author to hurry his thoroughly interesting hero off the scene in a few nervous paragraphs. But even this is no serious defect, for the general impression must be maintained ; a prolonged soft orchestral strain for Little Billee would be mere sentiment, and episodic, the significance of " Trilby " having ended in Trilby's dying with the wrong name upon her lips. Every part of the wonderful story is unconsciously managed with artistic reference to the whole ; its incidents are as rich in meaning as you care to consider them. Trilby opens her heart to the Laird, and is most lover-like with him who is most brotherly. Her mother, poor lass, was an aristocrat with the bar sinister; her clerical father, a bibulous character enchantingly outlined, was her only authority for her disbelief in dogma. No stress is laid on these characteristics and conditions; but they tell. Taffy preserves an English silence when Gecko speaks his soulful and spills over. You half resent the hearty postlude, through your own too acute memory of what is past. Yet the book was bound to end in a *tempo primo*, in a strain of peace and hope as like as possible to what was hushed forever, the jocund dance-measure of art and friendship and Latin-Quarter youth. For "Trilby" is comedy, after all, genuine comedy, and it is so to be named, albeit with a scandalous lump in the throat. As it is, we take it; we covet it; we will pay any price for it; we cannot get along without it. "*Je prong!*"

Mr. Du Maurier is not the first artist in England who has come over the border into literature with victorious results. Opie and Fuseli were among the most suggestive of thinkers and talkers; Sir Joshua lectured with academic vigor and graceful persuasiveness; Haydon had an almost unequalled eye for character, and a racy, biting, individual manner with his pen. But no artist has so endowed the world of romance. Mr. Du Maurier's achievement is not of malice prepense. As Dian stole to Endymion sleeping, so has immortal luck come upon him, chiefly because he did not, like the misguided Imlac in "Rasselas," "determine to become" — a classic. "Trilby," born of leisure and pastime, is vagrant; heedless of means to the end; profoundly modest and simple; told for what it is worth, as if it were, at least, something real and dear to the teller. Out of this easy, pleasure-giving mood, from one who is no trained expert, who has no idea to broach of disturbance or reform, out of genial genius, in short, which hates the niggardly hand and scatters roses, comes a gift of unique beauty. It crowns the publishers' year, as do "Lord Ormont and his Aminta," "Perleycross," and "The Jungle Book." With these great works of great writers, it stands, oddly enough, as tall as any; fresh, wide, healthful, curative, like them; and like them, a terrible punch on the head to a hundred little puling contemporane-

"Trilby"

ous novels, with their crude and cowardly theories of life.

The "Trilby" pictures, haphazard and effectual as is their text, can bear no more direct praise than that they are verily Mr. Du Maurier's. The masterly grouping, the multitude of fine lines, the spirited perspective, are here as of old. Some of these illustrations, not necessarily the best, stay on the retina; among such, surely, is the ludicrous, dripping funeral procession of the landlady's vernacular lie; that huge procession filing up-street, with one belated, civic infant on the reviewing-stand! Hardly second to it as a spectacle is the high-born rogue of a Zouave, enacting the trussed fowl at midnight on the studio floor, or the companion gem, set in the dubious out-of-doors of the great original Parisian Carry-hatide. Of the serious drawings, there is a memorable one among the three of Trilby singing, with her delicately advanced foot, and falling hair, and the luminous Ellen-Terry-like look in her kind eyes. Above all, who can forget the pathetic, pleading figure of the little boy Jeannot, in his pretty Palm Sunday clothes, losing his holiday, losing faith in his sister; and of Trilby over him, revoking her promise, and compassing what was in very truth the "meanest and lowest deed" of her brief, unselfish life? She cried herself to sleep often, remembering it, but to Mrs. Bagot it was monstrous trivial: "the putting-off of a small child." Her too typical phrase, "wrong with the intense wrongness of a right-minded person," as Ruskin says, gives you a pang. So does the inscription under the last glimpse we have of Little Billee, poignant enough without the "*Quae nunc abibis in loca*," which rushes its sweet pagan heart-break into the Rector's mind. In these casual intolerable thrusts deep into the nerve of laughter or of tears, Mr. Du Maurier demonstrates his right of authorship; these, and not vain verbal felicities, constitute his literary style.

Modern Laodicea
By
Norman Hapgood

MODERN LAODICEA

FOR centuries the word Laodicean was a reproach; to-day it is beginning to carry with it a suggestion of nobility. It was Saint John who, in making the unknown city famous, covered it with obloquy:

"And unto the angel of the church of the Laodiceans write: . . .

"'I know thy works, that thou art neither cold nor hot: I would thou wert cold or hot.

"'So, then, because thou art lukewarm, and neither cold nor hot, I will spew thee out of my mouth.'"

Among the moderns who have suggested that to be neither hot nor cold is to be well, Mr. Thomas Hardy is prominent, as he gave the title of "A Laodicean" to a novel of which the heroine is attractive. She is a girl who loves both the old and the new where they are most in conflict. She liked ruins and she liked restorations. She had half a mind to marry a picturesque noble, De Stancy, with no brains, no character, and an atmosphere of old-world romance, and she did marry a hard-headed modern. At the end of the book, she remarks : " 'We'll build a new house beside the ruin, and show the modern spirit forevermore . . . but, George, I wish —' And Paula repressed a sigh.

" ' Well ? '

" ' I wish my castle was not burned ; and I wish you were a De Stancy.' "

At Harvard University, a few years ago, there was started a society intended to represent the true spirit of the Neo-Laodiceans. It held that lukewarmness was the most admirable condition obtainable by man. Moral heat or cold in the heart of any applicant for election was reason for his rejection. "Nothing in excess" was suggested as a motto, but the word "but" was thought to be a more subtle suggestion that something could always be said on either side. In the end no motto was chosen, because this matter, like all other matters, was not pressed. For refreshments, lukewarm tea and sweet California wine were served. Conversation was neither encouraged nor discouraged. Serious argument was as freely tolerated as genuine trifling. A well-known man in college, who thought himself worthy of the club, was rejected because he was believed to be hostile to seriousness. Another was kept out because, although he said nothing against frivolity, it bored him.

The society had no secrets. The members sought no proselytes, but gave full answers to all inquiries. The Harvard students smiled and were interested. The young women at the Harvard Annex tried to laugh, but thought it was n't right. They said the young men were posing. The most magnanimous said that under the seemingly erroneous spirit was a really ardent search for truth. The Annex held but one girl who was ever mentioned for membership, and she was defeated by a close vote on the ground that, although her Laodiceanism seemed perfect, as she was a woman it was axiomatic that a thorough knowledge of her would reveal some ethical prejudice.

The founder of the society, naturally enough, was the most imperfect member. At one time there was serious thought of accepting his resignation. Instead of being lukewarm he was alternately hot and cold, being one of the ablest moral speakers as well as one of the most inspired jesters at morality. He himself did not know whether reverence or blasphemy was strongest in him. It was the perfection of this doubt about himself which induced the club to forgive his unstable equilibrium.

"Doing is a deadly thing; doing ends in death." One member was expelled because he quoted with approval this Antinomian hymn. That statement is as far from improved Laodiceanism as is the fury for doing things. Action is well enough if it be within bounds, as is rest. The Laodicean must see the advantages of all opposites, else he is unworthy of his name.

In contrast to the founder was the elected head of the society, the most fully developed specimen, a model of intellectual and temperamental moderation. He was mild in study, in exercise, in personal relations. He had more wisdom than most men and more knowledge, but he had acquired his knowledge, not by effort, but by putting his attention, when he chose to give attention to the acquisition of facts, to those of permanent importance. He had never wasted any strength on hobbies; he had never been enthusiastic. Yet he had always been interested. He knew nothing that was not worth knowing. His easy intellectual spirit was combined with æsthetic fineness and sensuous delicacy. He spent much of his time in the sunshine, amusing himself with the passing events of the hour. His friends were chosen for their dispositions, not for their acquirements. He preferred a small mind, simple and harmonious, to a large one distorted or turbulent. He spent a few hours of the day in severe study, a few in strolling in the air, a few in chatting and drinking tea, a few in reading poetry or other imaginative literature. He was fond of conversation, but not of dispute. He was loyal to reason and cared little for reasoning.

Between these two types lay the other five members, Laodiceans of varying degrees. One was looked upon as of doubtful standing on account of his temperament, which seemed to belong to the land of Far Niente, with which we had no desire to be allied. He was lazy, and he kept his membership only because of his intellectual fairness. His organs were partial to rest, but his mind was judicial and regretted the defect of his temperament. As his approval was distributed impartially among the alert and the sleepy, the faithful and the unbelieving, we let his ideas atone for his instincts.

The others, who were not especially distinct types, were good average examples of the species. In addition, we had seven honorary members. There was a rule that no man in his lifetime could be an honorary member, but there was one living man so deserving of the honor that we did all we could within the letter of the rule: we voted that Arthur James Balfour should acquire a membership immediately upon his death. He was the only man who received this tribute. Among the dead, Omar Khayyam was elected, with one dissent, on the ground that the Persian poet was injudiciously opposed to virtue; and Socrates, Lucretius, Horace, Goethe, and Molière passed without challenge. Over Lucretia Borgia, who was proposed by the founder, there was a long fight, with the same objections that had been made against him. On the plea that she was as fond of virtue as of vice we admitted her, though with regret.

Since the second gathering, though two years have passed, the club has not met, simply because no one has suggested a meeting. This is thought to be in keeping with its principles. I have gone thus fully into its history because it is the only organized representation of the principles of the new sect. These principles, though not yet exactly defined, are shadowed forth in the belief of these seven youths. They were confident, at the time, that the true Laodicea would grow in size and in respect. It could never number many, because by the nature of its creed it was an intellectual aristocracy; but it would grow slowly larger as the course of evolution brought the world gradually nearer to the summit of development. Whether most of us persist in this belief, I do not know. Nor do I know whether most of us believe still that in a world where almost everybody is vociferously supporting one side of every question it is a pleasant thing to sit in the shade, to drink lukewarm nourishment, and to say sweetly that there is some good on either side. There may be a better course than this — and there may not.

The Intellectual Parvenu
By
Norman Hapgood

THE INTELLECTUAL PARVENU

AT a time when so many new ideas about the humanities are flooding America it is not surprising that among our ambitious and intelligent young men of the first generation of culture are many whose intellectual methods show more eagerness than measure. With no traditions behind them they do not realize how necessary are humility, repose, and care to sound ripening of the perceptions and the judgment. As their fathers struggled for academic education and for material ease, the sons make a struggle and an excitement of ideas on art. They over-emphasize what they get hold of, from a deficient sense of permanent values. Though this spectacle has been seen at other times, probably never before was so large a mass of new ideas thrown to so hungry a public.

The men of whom I speak are more occupied with the idea of enlightenment than with the things which give light. Americans give too much importance to intellectual things, it is frequently said.

The Intellectual Parvenu

Riper intelligence puts less emphasis on itself. When we first see beyond others about us we are dazzled by the idea of our own advancement. Because we have discarded some errors or removed some ignorance we rejoice in our grasp of truth. This often makes us set ourselves up as enemies of the Philistines and of all their ways. Seeing the futility of their labor we assume opinions on subjects over which we have not labored. Seeing the uselessness of much acquired fact we are content with superficial knowledge. We smile in satisfaction over the radicalness of our point of view, and because we know the deadness of some conventions we think that a thing is true because it is new. The established is commonplace. What is known to all or felt by all is unimportant. Distinction consists in seeing and believing novel things.

> "I. the heir of all the ages
> In the foremost files of time."

Most often these victims of their own progress are our college men. Indeed in a confused way the mass of our half-educated people who distrust the influences of our colleges have such products in their minds. Of course, however, the fault is not with our institutions, but with a hasty civilization. In an American college to-day altogether too much interest is taken in shallow modernity, but our colleges, on the whole, send their students away with less of the bigotry of new knowledge than they had on entrance. Steadily assertion of intellectual heterodoxy, contempt for the conventional, is becoming less a source of general interest in our educational institution; steadily it is coming to be seen as a crudity. So many youths have flaunted end-of-the-century banners that the device is already almost worthless, and it is not so much the graduate of to-morrow as the graduate of ten years ago, who is the centre of the admiring little circle which pins its faith in an enlightened life on some arbitrary and confident preacher of new things. The gospel of the prophet may be Japanese art; it may be the necessity of living in Europe; or it may be the futility of thinking anything is better than anything else. This American phenomenon is found in abundance in all of our cities, but if he can get away he lives in an European art centre, an essential part of no life except that of his apostles.

That these persons may be regarded as a class is

proved by their surprising agreement of opinion. For instance, of the young art prophets whom I know, all Americans, some living in Europe, some by necessity in America, every one thinks that the others are so shallow that what influence they have is surprising; each thinks that the only art of to-day is French or Japanese; that there has never been any art in England; that the most advanced literature of the world is the realism of the younger men in Paris; that Oscar Wilde is the most intelligent of British writers; that the admiration of Shakespeare is a superstition; that there is much less beauty in nature than in art; that work in any unartistic employment is a waste of life; and that it is impossible for an intelligent man to be contented in America. When so many radical ideas are held in common there must be some way of generalizing about the individuals holding them. They are alike, also, not only in their opinions, but in their fields of ignorance. They are fond of talking about atavism, for instance, and cannot state exactly any one of the conflicting theories of heredity. They ostensibly treat art scientifically, psychologically, and do not know the simplest facts of experimental physiological psychology. They generalize about movements and periods after reading a few books about each. The saying that the French would be the best cooks in Europe if they had any butcher's meat, modified by Mr. Bagehot into the aphorism that they would be the best writers of the day if they had anything to say, applies also to these critics who make such striking theories out of so little. They accuse of ignorance all who lack knowledge in their fields; all knowledge outside of their field they look upon as pedantry.

Salient, however, as are the weaknesses of these unformed prophets they do have their attractive side. They have enthusiasm about things of the mind, they have indignation for what they deem Philistinism, and with their love of prominence in the world of ideas is mixed some genuine respect for truth. Are our American workers in the world of ideas to be permanently open to the charge of over-emphasis, of lacking distinction, finish, wholeness? Most of us believe not. We believe that the prominence of cleverness, rather than of soundness, just now is a temporary thing, like our social crudities, from which later the powers of a race will free themselves.

In the meantime, we have in an impressive form

the first crop of the literature of the future. Journals are founded all over the country which, in an average life of a few months, express the opinions and reveal the art of a few young men who think they are ahead of their times. Just now the main characteristic of this literature is that it suggests as often as it can the art of painting. It calls itself by the name of a color — yellow, green, purple, gray. Constant use is made of the slang of art. Indeed their only way of appearing artistic seems to be to make their writing as far as possible remind the reader of the plastic arts. Art is ostentatiously opposed to everything else, especially to scholarship, morality, and industry. The idea seems to be that art is made by talking about art, or by talking about life in terms of art. Equally noticeable is the instinct that in making one special quality conspicuous by neglecting others, they are showing originality. They do not see that in an artist great enough to give a large man the feeling of life there are too many elements for any detail to be conspicuous. The work of this artist will be life-like; commonplace, unless seen by an eye to which common life reveals its interests. Edmond de Goncourt can see nothing in "The

Scandinavian Hamlet." He prefers Père Goriot, who is newer, he thinks, and more real. Edmond de Goncourt is an admirable example of the attitude of a few men in Paris who have largely influenced some of our tawdry literature. In one of his journals he remarks sadly that in a certain conversation about abstract things, general human points of view, he failed to shine, and he asks plaintively why it is that men who "on all other subjects" find original things to say are in these generalities on a footing with the rest of the world, — which means to him, flat. Readers of the eight volumes of the journal may smile at the "all other subjects," but it is at least true that on certain narrow topics of which few persons know anything he could feel more profound than he could on subjects of universal human interest. His test of Shakespeare, by the way, is an apt one. It does not condemn a man that he does not find Hamlet interesting. Many intelligent men do not. Any man, however, who infers, from his lack of appreciation, that Shakespeare is not a great artist is deficient in critical intelligence and in understanding of the value of evidence. And when a man remarks that Raphael, Beethoven, or Shakespeare, was a great man in his time, but that the world has progressed, and that, as we stand on the shoulders of our predecessors, the Balzac of this century sees more than the Shakespeare of two centuries earlier, we have a subject for comedy. Artists, except the very highest, are likely to be as critics arbitrary and intolerant, though often acute and original, and these hangers-on of the art-world have the arbitrariness without the compensating exact knowledge.

That any critic who seriously treats with contempt any man or any institution that has a high place in the general world of ideas is shallow, an avoider and not a solver of questions which confront a man of mature culture and broad mind, is almost axiomatic. When we hear so many critics to-day expressing scorn of whole nations, saying of England, perhaps, that she has no art, of Germany, that she has only dull learning, of America that she is Philistine ; when we see these critics surrounded by groups of followers, do we not wish, with some reason, that we had a Molière to-day ? What a play he could make of "Les Critiques Ridicules;" or of "L'Ecole des Aesthètes," or of "L'Américain Malgré Lui." The poems of Mr. Gilbert and of Punch are pleasing within their range, but the subject deserves to be treated in one of the world's comedies. The scientific art criticism of men who know of art and science nothing except the jargon makes one sometimes doubt the value of the general spread of ideas. Lombroso, Nordau, even parts of Spencer, not to speak of the mass of inferior generalizing of wide scope, would have brought a sad smile to the face of the real scientist who spent seven years studying earth-worms alone.

The School of Jingoes
By
Thomas Wentworth Higginson

THE SCHOOL OF JINGOES

IN a certain colored regiment there was a chaplain who was habitually called by the negroes, with their usual gift at lucky misnomers, "Mr. Chapman." He was very fond of risky adventures, and one of the negroes once said: "Woffor Mas' Chapman made preacher fo'? He's de fightin'est mos' Yankee I ebber see in all my days!" It is impossible not to read this in reading what is written by these friends of peace, who are constantly using the olive branch for a war club and hammering away at those who think differently. The excellent Mr. Angell, in the last number of "Our Dark Friends," announces in one column that the object of his paper is "the humane education of the millions," and in another column that it is to be wished "that England had not only Venezuela, but every other Spanish-speaking colony on the face of the earth." In this manner, more prosaically, do Mr. Edward Atkinson and Mr. Edward D. Mead hold it up as the highest desideratum for every part of Spanish and Portuguese America to pass into English hands. Grant the force of all their arguments, can this be regarded as the gospel of serenity and brotherly love? It rather recalls Heine's glowing description of one of his early teachers, one Schramm, who had written a book on Universal Peace, and in whose classes the boys pommelled each other with especial vigor.

If jingoism there be on earth, where are its headquarters, its normal school, its university extension system? Where, pray, but in the example of England? No one who has watched the course of things at Washington can help seeing the influence of that vast object-lesson. Seeley's book, "The Expansion of England," is of itself enough to demoralize a whole generation of Congressmen. It is the trophies of Great Britain which will not allow Lodge and Roosevelt to sleep. Logically, they have the right of it. If it be a great and beneficent thing for England to annex, by hook or crook, every desirable harbor or island on the globe; to secure Gibraltar by a trick, India by a lucky disobedience of orders, Egypt by a temporary occupation of which the other end never arrives, — why not follow the example? This impulse lay behind the whole Hawaiian negotiation; it asserts itself in all the Venezuela interference, in all the Cuban imbroglio. Moreover, it is absolutely consistent and defensible, if England is, as we are constantly assured, the great, beneficent, and civilizing power on the earth. If so, let us also be beneficent; let us proceed to civilize; let us, too, say, especially to all Spanish-speaking peoples, "Sois mon frère, ou je te tue!"

If there ever was a Church Militant, surely England is the Nation Militant. While we debate a gunboat, she equips a fleet; while we introduce a bill for an earth-work, and refer it to a committee, she forwards ten additional guns to Puget Sound. "Her march is o'er the mountain wave," as Campbell long since boasted; and yet, whenever the youngest statesman asks why we should not be allowed to take a faltering step after her, he is treated as if he had violated the traditions of the human race and had indeed brought death into the world and all our woe. Let us at heart be consistent. To me, I confess, the old tradition of "an unarmed nation" — about which that good soldier, Gen. F. A. Walker, once made so fine an address — still seems the better thing. But the unarmed nation is the condemnation of

England; if defencelessness is right, then England is all wrong, and we should say so. We can by no possible combination be English and pacific at the same time.

Above all, it seems to me an absolute abandonment of the whole principle of republican institutions to say that they are for one nation alone, and for only those who speak one language. If deserving means anything, it means that sooner or later all will grow up to it. Nobody doubts that the Romans governed well and were the best road-builders on this planet; but all now admit that it helped human progress when they took themselves out of England and left those warring tribes to work themselves out of their dark condition into such self-government as they now possess. There was a time on this continent when Mexico was such a scene of chaos that the very word "to Mexicanize" carried a meaning of disorder. Yet what State of the Union has shown more definite and encouraging progress than has been accomplished in Mexico within the last ten years? What Mexico is, every Spanish-American or Portuguese-American state may yet be, only give it time and a fair chance. If we believe that the principle of self-government is unavailable for those who speak Spanish, we might as well have allowed Maximilian to set up his little empire undisturbed. No one ever doubted that Louis Napoleon knew how to build good roads and to shoot straight; and perhaps he might have taught the same arts to his representative. Whatever injury we may before have done to Mexico, we repaid it liberally when we said to Europe, ;" Hands off," and secured to that Spanish-American state its splendid career of self-development out of chaos. What Mexico has done the states of South America may yet imitate.

The Uses of Perversity
By
Laurence Jerrold

THE USES OF PERVERSITY.

HERE French must lend its subtler and more penetrating aroma. A stronger spice must brace the good old English toned-down flavor. The word must be supposed invigorated, for the thing it is to mean is forcible. Waywardness is not the humor of this perversity, and it has more of the perverted than of the perverse. Surface hits at cussedness, facile thrusts at contrariness, leave it unscathed; for it goes deeper than whimsicality and underlies the quaintness sharp wit picks out of little things gone wrong. Perversity, thus for a space restored to its unemasculated meaning, is a twisted distortion of root and branch, not a gentle deflection of airy twigs. To paint a French thing the word must assume a Gallic hue, and as the thing is deep-dyed, so the word must borrow for the nonce a fuller tone.

Words, indeed, are but things. The names on which French thought has thrived have been true tokens of its moods, and word-changes have meant revolutions of fact, for the facts here are the words.

The Uses of Perversity

Realism worsting Romanticism, the newest Decadence undoing Realism, are evolutions in speech which cover a progression in life. The sentimentality of Art meant gush in practice and the attitudes of literature were struck in reality. Dissection in fiction argued an actual habit of analysis, and materiality was most lived for when it was most written about. The reaction in words has ushered in a revolution of fact, or, what comes to the same, the new literature has sprung from the new life. From paroxysm to anti-climax has been the way of this parallel progression, as it is of every change. The pendulum has swayed from Realism and struck the opposite beam. But the earth turned while we swung, and we have landed, not on Romance again, whence we had leaped to Realism, but on Perversity, whence a lucky spring may eventually set us down on something wiser and better. Yet there are books in the running brooks, and there may be sermons in even the troubled streams that water this new land of our discovery. The inner reaction in men and things which the outer anti-climax of names and words betokens is no barren waste, and yields experience a plentiful harvest. The fruits are not seldom ill-flavored, but

By Laurence Jerrold

the flavor is strong, and the uses of this new perversity are not insipid, though they be but bittersweet.

Idealism is our perversion, and the Soul depraves us. We are drinking the dregs of the immaterial and have touched the dingiest bottoms of purity. The relativity of the object has turned our heads, and we are soul-mad. Apotheosis of soul and annihilation of body, the only seemly pegs on which well-thinking "jeunes" can now hang their periods, which once the bait-hook of "analytical observation" alone could catch, are the principles of our disintegration. Their work is swift, for the fear of lagging in the race for modernity speeds it, and it is wholesale. Nature and common-sense crumble, and sincerity has long since withered away. Cabaret conversations are of the stupidity of sex, and small-talk in drawing-rooms runs on the idiocy of love. Mating is a platitude, begetting an absurdity, and motherhood has the quaintness of things obsolete. The abolition of sex is the new crusade, and the last religion is of the future, when the aristocracy of the intellect shall, Jupiter-like, eschew animality, and engender its children in a thought. Literature foretells the time, and art paints the soul with daring straightforwardness on canvas, using microscopic brushes dipped in gold and devoting years to the task, for psychic delineation is minute and precious.

Soul gives form, and the ethereal must take outward shape. Hence the new attitude. A virginal appearance and the candor of an "enfant de chœur" are its necessary conditions. The hair, dark for women, preferably golden for men, is long, forlorn, and parted. Complexions are of wax when feminine; when masculine, of pale peach-blossom! A cherub's smile plays on the lips, and eyes must, within the bounds of feasibility, show the vacuity of an infant's. In voice and gesture, being more easily practised, is the new puerility most felicitously expressed. The secret lies in the suppression of both. The voice must be "white," and every accent, every shade of tone that gives but the faint image of a color, is a flaw. A still grosser imperfection would be aught of hasty or unmeasured in gesture or movement. In small-talk anent the Soul, as in the impressive elocution of nursery rhymes, carnal oblivion must be insured by immovableness of limb, and further than the uplifting of a finger the soulful do not venture. The golden-haired youth, lisping with the "voix blanche" of white-robed "premières communiantes," pictures the perversion of purity.

As at once a sign of health and a stigma of decay there comes amid this struggling for a Soul the fitful yet eventual triumph of the flesh. The trampled body turns and fells its oppressors, and this is Nature's victory, claiming, after all, her own. But it is also Nature's revenge, for she bestows not of her best on those who have spurned the boon, and her gifts are cruel to her prodigal sons. Passion is vouchsafed generously anew to some few who abjured it, but it has to pay its penalty. The actress who (not for respectability's sake — this care is unknown in her Bohemia — but as a tribute to the new perversion) had renounced the flesh, and the poet who had made dying all the rage and relegated mere living to the lumber-room, have to screen the simplest of idyls, not from the stare of the Puritan, but from the prying of the last decadence. More often a yet heavier penalty is paid. The flesh will out, and, stifled by the perversion of purity, breaks impurely forth. The fat little Marseillais poet who may be heard of an evening in his popular part of the prophet of the new renunciation anathematizing the scurrility of sex and execrating the ugliness of love, the golden-haired painter whose boast is his choir-boy appearance, are rivals in innuendo and salaciousness when the work of life is over and play-hours begin. In the daytime even the test of a bottle of champagne or of but a half pint of beer is one the new purity will hardly stand. The slender youth whom you have heard preaching the gospel of asceticism amid a circle of amused and half-deceived ladies goes with you to sip a "quart" at the Café de la Place Blanche, upstairs, and shows surprising intimacy with the feminine element of that particular world, and no little experience of fleshly doctrines.

The uses of perversity wander wide in seriousness and in theory, and return to Nature in practice and at play. But the return is by a yet muddier way than the digression, and a cleaner and wholesomer path must be opened up before the straight line can be struck again.

A Comment on Some
   Recent Books
By
Hamilton Wright Mabie

A COMMENT ON SOME RECENT BOOKS

SITTING in slippered ease before the fire, in that ripe hour when the violence of flame has given place to a calm and penetrating glow, one hears the wind without as if it were a tumult in some other world. The great waves of sound follow each other in swift succession, but they break and wreck themselves on a shore so remote that one meditates unconcerned in the warmth of the wide-throated chimney. The sense of repose and ease within is too deep to be disturbed by the roar that fills the wintry night without. And yet how fragile are the walls that guard our glowing comfort from the storm of the vast world, and how small a space of light and heat is ours in the great sweep of elemental forces!

The policing of the world and the suppression of the cut-throat and the savage secure, at times, an order so pervasive and so stable that we forgot the possibilities of revolt and tragedy which underlie human society in its most serene as in its most agitated moments. The elemental forces which plant the seeds of tragedy in every human life, play as freely and powerfully through society to-day as in those turbulent periods when strong natures made laws for themselves and gave full vent to individual impulse. As a rule, these forces expend themselves in well-defined and orderly channels; but they have lost nothing of their old destructiveness if for any reason they leave these channels or overflow their narrow courses. Conventions are more rigidly enforced and more widely accepted to-day than ever before; but the tide of life is as deep and full and swift as of old, and when its current is set it sweeps conventions before it as fragile piers are torn up and washed out by furious seas.

In our slippered ease, protected by orderly government, by written constitutions, by a police who are always in evidence, we sometimes forget of what perilous stuff we are made, and how inseparable from human life are those elements of tragedy which from time to time startle us in our repose, and make us aware that the most awful pages of history may be rewritten in the record of our own day. It will be a dull day if the time ever comes when uncertainty and peril are banished from the life of men. When the seas are no longer tossed by storms, the joy and the training of eye, hand, and heart in seamanship will go out. The antique virtues of courage, endurance, and high-hearted sacrifice cannot perish without the loss of that which makes it worth while to live; but these qualities, which give heroic fibre to character, cannot be developed if danger and uncertainty are to be banished from human experience. A stable world is essential to progress, but a world without the element of peril would comfort the body and destroy the soul. In some form the temper of the adventurer, the explorer, the sailor, and the soldier must be preserved in an orderly and peaceful society; that sluggish stability for which business interests are always praying would make money abundant, but impoverish the money-getters. There would be nothing worth buying in a community in which men were no longer tempted and life had no longer that interest which grows out of its dramatic possibilities.

That order ought to grow, and will grow, is the conviction of all who believe in progress; but society will be preserved from stagnation by the fact that every man who comes into the world brings with him all the possibilities which the first man brought. For men are born, not made, in spite of all our superior mechanism; and although a man is born to-day into conditions more favorable to acceptance and growth than to rejection and revolt, he must still solve his personal problem as in the stormier ages, and make his own adjustment to his time. And in the making of that adjustment lie all the elements of the human tragedy. The policing of the world will grow more complete from age to age, but every man born into this established order will bring with him the perilous stuff of revolt and revolution. Without this background of tragic possibility life would lose that perpetual spell which it casts upon the artistic spirit in every generation; it would cease to be the drama to which a thousand pens have striven to give form, before which a thousand thousand spectators have sat in a silence more affecting than the most rapturous tumult of applause.

In these "piping times of peace" perhaps the artist renders no greater service to his kind than by keeping the tragic background of life in clear view. Men sorely need to be reminded of the immeasurable space which surrounds them and the bottomless gulfs which open beneath them. In this trafficking age, when so many slowly or swiftly coin strength, time, and joy into money, the constant vision of the human drama, with its deep and fruitful suggestiveness, is a necessity, and it can hardly be a matter of coincidence that the tragic side of the drama has so strongly appealed to men of artistic temper in recent years. Whatever may be said about the sanity of view and of art of Flaubert, Zola, and De Maupassant; of Ibsen and Maeterlinck; of George Moore, William Sharp, and the group of younger writers who, with varying degrees of success, are breaking from the beaten paths, it is certain that they have laid bare the primitive elements in the human problem. The dramas of Ibsen and Maeterlinck have brought not peace but a sword into recent discussion of the province and nature of art; but whatever may be our judgment of the truth and quality of these end-of-the-century readings and renderings of the great drama, there is no question about their departure from the conventional point of view. They may be partial, even misleading, in the interpretation of life and its meaning which they suggest, but they disturb and agitate us; they make us realize how fragile are the structures which so many men and women build over the abysses. If they do nothing more than irritate us, they render us a service; for irritation is better than the repose of unconsciousness; it brings us back to the sense of life; it makes us aware of the deeper realities.

Mr. Sharp's "Vistas" seems at first reading a book out of another century, so dominant is its tragic note, so remote its themes, so elemental its consciousness. It is a book of glimpses only; but these glimpses open up the recesses and obscurities where destiny is swiftly or slowly shaped. Lawmaking and the police seem very superficial assurances and guardians of order in a world in which, beyond their ken or reach, such tremendous forces of good and evil are slumbering; traffic and finance seem matters of secondary interest or occupation when such passions are stirring and striving. And yet "Vistas" is peculiarly a book of our time; it registers the revolt which the man of insight and artistic temper always makes when conventions begin to cut to the quick, and the air becomes close and heavy. The human spirit must have room and sweep; it must feel continually the great forces which play through it; it must carry with it the continual consciousness of its possibilities of good and evil. And the more orderly society becomes the greater will be the need of keeping alive the sense of peril and uncertainty from forces which may be quiescent but which are never dead ; of remembering that there must be freedom as well as restraint, and that the policeman must represent an order which is accepted as well as enforced.

The dramatists and the novelists continually shatter our sense of security by reminding us that if Arthur Dimmesdale is dead, Philip Christian survives ; that if Isolde has perished, Anna Karenina still lives; that if Francesca da Rimini is no longer swept by the relentless blasts, Tess is not less tragically borne on to her doom. The commonplace man sees the commonplace so constantly that he needs in every age his kinsman of keener sight and finer spirit to remind him that life is not in things ; and that neither peace for traffic nor order for quietness of mind is its supreme end. And, after all, the singing of the open fire is the sweeter for the tumult beyond the walls.

One Word More
By
Hamilton Wright Mabie

ONE WORD MORE

THE contemporary writing which is commonly called "decadent" has one quality which is likely to be fatal to its permanence, — it wears out the reader's interest. On the first reading it has a certain newness of manner, a certain unconventionality of form and idea, which catch the attention; but these qualties catch the attention, they do not hold it; with each successive reading the spell weakens until it is largely spent. We discover that the manner which caught us, so to speak, at the start, is either self-conscious or tricky; and both qualities are fatal to permanence. There is nothing so inimical to the highest success in art as self-consciousness, and nothing is so soon discovered as a trick of style. It is, of course, both unintelligent and idle to characterize a considerable mass of writing in general terms; but, even with such differences of insight and ability as the decadent literature reveals, it has certain characteristics in common, and these characteristics disclose its essential qualities. They are significant enough to furnish a basis for a dispassionate opinion.

With the revolt against the conventional and the commonplace, especially on the part of the youngest men, every lover of sound writing must be heartily in sympathy. In a time when Edwin Arnold, Alfred Austin, and Lewis Morris are gravely brought forward as fit candidates for the laureateship which Wordsworth and Tennyson held in succession, it is not surprising that young men with a real feeling for literature fall to cursing and take refuge in eccentricity of all kinds. It must frankly be confessed that a great deal of current writing, while uncommonly good as regards form and taste, is devoid of anything approaching freshness of feeling or originality of idea. Its prime characteristic is well-bred, well-dressed, and well-mannered mediocrity ; of contact with life it gives no faintest evidence ; of imagination, passion, and feeling — those prime qualities out of which great literature is compounded — it is as innocent as the average Sunday-Shool publication. It is not without form, but it is utterly void.

That men who are conscious, even in a blind

CHAP-BOOK ESSAYS
By Hamilton W. Mabie

way, of the tragic elements of life should revolt against this widespread dominion of the commonplace is matter neither for astonishment nor regret; if they have blood in their veins and vitality in their brains, they cannot do otherwise. The responsibility for excesses and eccentricities generally rests with the conditions which have set the reaction in motion. When men begin to suffocate, windows are likely to be broken as well as opened; when Philistia waxes prosperous and boastful, Bohemia receives sudden and notable accessions of population.

Among English-speaking people at least, it is chiefly as a reaction that decadent literature is significant. It is an attempt to get away from the mortal dulness of the mass of contemporary writing, — an effort to see life anew and feel it afresh. In many cases, it is, however, mistaken not only in morals, but in method : it confuses mannerism with originality, and unconventionality with power. A manner may be novel and, at the same time, bad; one may be unconventional and, at the same time, essentially weak. In moments of hot and righteous indignation a little cursing of the right sort may be pardonable ; but cursing has no lasting quality.

A revolt against too many clothes, or against a deadly uniformity of cut and style, is always justifiable; but nudity is not the only alternative; there is an intermediate position in which one may be both clothed *and* in his right mind.

Now, there is nothing more certain than that the originality of the greater and more enduring books is free from self-consciousness, mannerism, and eccentricity in any form. As a rule, the greater the work the greater the difficulty of classifying it, of putting one's hand on the secret of its charm, of describing it in a phrase. The contrast between Shakespeare and Maeterlinck is, in this respect, so striking that one wonders how the admirers of the gifted Belgian were led into the blunder of forcing it upon contemporary readers. Maeterlinck has unmistakable power; his skill in introducing atmospheric effects, in assailing the senses of his readers without awakening their consciousness that powerful influences are in the air, his genius in the use of suggestion, are evident almost at a glance. But when one has read "The Intruder" or "The Princess Maleine" one has, in a way, read all these powerful and intensely individual dramas. They are all worked out by a single method, and that method is instantly detected. Maeterlinck's manner is so obvious that no one can overlook or mistake it. With Shakespeare, on the other hand, there is the greatest difficulty in discovering any manner at all. At his best Shakespeare is magical ; there is no getting at his way of doing things. His method is so free, so natural, so varied, and moves along such simple lines that we take it for granted, as if it were a part of the order of things. There is a kind of elemental unconsciousness in him which gives his artistic processes the apparent ease, the fulness, and range of the processes of nature.

"The great merit, it seems to me," writes Mr. Lowell to Professor Norton, "of the old painters was that they did not try to be original. 'To say a thing,' says Goethe, 'that everybody else has said before, as quietly as if nobody had ever said it, *that* is originality.'" In other words, originality consists not in saying new things, but in saying true things. It is for this reason that the great writers have no surprises for us ; they lift into the light of clear expression things that have lain silent at the bottom of our natures ; things profoundly felt, but never spoken. In like manner, originality in form and style is not a matter of novelty, but of deeper feeling and surer touch. A piece of work which, like a popular song, has a rhythm or manner which catches the senses, may have a lusty life, but is certain to have a brief one. There is nothing "catching" or striking, in the superficial sense, in the greater works of art. Their very simplicity hides their superiority, and the world makes acquaintance with them very slowly.

A genuine reaction, of the kind which predicts a true liberation of the imagination, is only momentarily a revolt against outgrown methods and the feebleness of a purely imitative art; it is essentially a return to the sources of power. It begins in revolt, but it does not long rest in that negative stage; it passes on to reconstruction, to creative work in a new and independent spirit. Goethe and Schiller went *through* the *Sturm and Drang* period; they did not stay in it. "The Sorrows of Werther" and "Goetz" were followed by "Tasso" and "Faust;" and "The Robbers" soon gave place to "William Tell." The Romanticists who made such an uproar when "Hernani" was put on the stage, did not long wear red waistcoats and flowing locks; they went to work and brought forth the solid fruits of genius.

The man on the barricade is a picturesque figure, but he must not stay too long or he becomes ridiculous; the insurrection, if it means anything, must issue in a permanent social or political order. Even genius will not redeem perpetual revolt from monotony, as the case of Byron clearly shows. Revolt is inspiring if it is the prelude to a new and better order; if it falls short of this achievement, it is only a disturbance of the peace. It means, in that case, that there is dissatisfaction, but that the reaction has no more real power than the tyranny or stupidity against which it takes up arms. The new impulse in literature, when it comes, will evidence its presence neither by indecency nor by eccentricity; but by a certain noble simplicity, by the sanity upon which a great authority always ultimately rests, by the clearness of its insight, and the depth of its sympathy with that deeper life of humanity, in which are the springs of originality and productiveness.

The Man Who Dares
By
Louise Chandler Moulton

THE MAN WHO DARES

"BALLADS AND SONGS," BY JOHN DAVIDSON

GRANT ALLEN has written of "The Woman Who Did" — and the title suggests that John Davidson may fitly be called "The Man Who Dares;" for certainly some of his themes and some of his lines, in this his latest book, are among the most daring in modern literature.

Richard Le Gallienne, in comparing William Watson and John Davidson, suggests that Davidson is a great man, and Watson a great manner. This is a statement I am not ready to indorse. I think Watson has much more than a great manner. He has noble and stately thought, a large outlook, and, in his own direction, subtle and keen perception. He knows the moods of the spirit, the reach of the soul; but the human heart does not cry out to him. He waits in the stately Court of the Intellect, and surveys the far heavens through its luminous windows.

Davidson, on the contrary, hearkens to the heart's cry. The passionate senses clamor in his lines.

The Man Who Dares

Ceaseless unrest assails him. Doubt and faith war in him for mastery. Above all he is human; and, secondly, he is modern. "Perfervid," "A Practical Novelist," and two or three other tales, at once merry and fantastic, prove his gifts as a story-teller. He has written several delightful plays, among which "Scaramouch In Naxos" is, perhaps, the most remarkable. Its originality, its charm, its wayward grace give it a place to itself in modern literature; and I doubt if we have any other man who could have given us quite the same thing. But when the right to careful attention of his other work has been fully admitted, I am inclined to think that nowhere does he more thoroughly prove his high claim to distinction than in his "Fleet-Street Eclogues," and his new volume of "Ballads and Songs."

Of all these Ballads the three that have most moved me are "A Ballad of a Nun," "A Ballad of Heaven," and "A Ballad of Hell." There is much crude strength in "A Ballad in Blank Verse of the Making of a Poet;" but the blank verse, impassioned though it be, has neither the stately splendor of Milton nor the artistic and finished grace of Tennyson. It is full of stress and strain, — this story of a youth who was brought up by a father and mother who really believed that the soul's probation ends with this brief span of earthly life, and that

" In life it is your privilege to choose,
But after death you have no choice at all."

He tortured his mother by his unbelief, until he slowly broke her heart, and " she died, in anguish for his sins." His father upbraided him, and he cried — very naturally, if not very poetically —

" Oh, let me be ! "

Then he sought his Aphrodite, and found her, dull, tawdry, unbeautiful, — an outcast of the streets. He wrote his dreams ; and then he felt that they were lies. He grew desperate, at last, and professed himself convicted of sin, and became a Christian — resolved to please his father, if he could not please himself. But this phase could not last; and he shattered his father's new-found happiness by a wild denunciation of all creeds, and an assertion that there is no God higher than ourselves. Then was the father torn between his desire to seek his wife in Heaven, and his impulse to go with his son into the jaws of Hell. At last, in his turn, the father died; and the poet — the child of storm and stress — was left at liberty to be himself —

> "—— a thoroughfare
> For all the pageantry of Time; to catch
> The mutterings of the Spirit of the Hour,
> And make them known."

There are lines, here and there, in this poem of exquisite beauty; but there are others that seem to me "tolerable and not to be endured."

I make my "Exodus From Houndsditch," without as yet being tempted to linger there, and come to "A Ballad of a Nun." And here, indeed, you have something of which only John Davidson has proved himself capable. The Ballad tells the old Roman Catholic legend of the Nun whom the lust of the flesh tempted.

There are stanzas here of such splendid power and beauty that they thrill one like noble and stirring music. You shall listen to some of them. The Abbess loved this Nun so well that she had trusted her above all the rest, and made her the Keeper of the Door: —

" High on a hill the Convent hung,
  Across a duchy looking down,
  Where everlasting mountains flung
  Their shadows over tower and town.

" The jewels of their lofty snows
  In constellations flashed at night ;
  Above their crests the moon arose ;
  The deep earth shuddered with delight.

" Long ere she left her cloudy bed,
  Still dreaming in the orient land,
  On many a mountain's happy head
  Dawn lightly laid her rosy hand.

" The adventurous sun took heaven by storm ;
  Clouds scattered largesses of rain ;
  The sounding cities, rich and warm,
  Smouldered and glittered in the plain.

" Sometimes it was a wandering wind,
  Sometimes the fragrance of the pine,
  Sometimes the thought how others sinned
  That turned her sweet blood into wine.

" Sometimes she heard a serenade
  Complaining sweetly, far away :
  She said, ' A young man wooes a maid ; '
  And dreamt of love till break of day."

In vain she plied her knotted scourge. Day after day she "had still the same red sin to purge." Winter came, and the snow shut in hill and plain; and she watched the nearest city glow beneath the frosty sky. "Her hungry heart devoured the town;" until, at last, she tore her fillet and veil into strips, and cast aside the ring and bracelet that she wore as the betrothed of Christ: —

> "'Life's dearest meaning I shall probe;
> Lo! I shall taste of love, at last!
> Away!' She doffed her outer robe,
> And sent it sailing down the blast.

> "Her body seemed to warm the wind;
> With bleeding feet o'er ice she ran;
> 'I leave the righteous God behind;
> I go to worship sinful man.'"

She reached "the sounding city's gate." She drank the wild cup of love to the dregs. She cried —

> "'I am sister to the mountains, now,
> And sister to the sun and moon.'"

She made her queen-like progress. She loved and lived —

"But soon her fire to ashes burned;
 Her beauty changed to haggardness;
 Her golden hair to silver turned;
 The hour came of her last caress.

"At midnight from her lonely bed
 She rose, and said, 'I have had my will.'
 The old ragged robe she donned, and fled
 Back to the convent on the hill."

She blessed, as she ran thither, the comfortable convent laws by which nuns who had sinned as she had done were buried alive. But I must copy the remaining stanzas, for no condensation can do justice to their tender, piteous, triumphant charm: —

"Like tired bells chiming in their sleep,
 The wind faint peals of laughter bore;
 She stopped her ears and climbed the steep,
 And thundered at the convent door.

"It opened straight: she entered in,
 And at the Wardress' feet fell prone:
 'I come to purge away my sin;
 Bury me, close me up in stone.'

"The Wardress raised her tenderly;
 She touched her wet and fast-shut eyes:

'Look, sister; sister, look at me;
  Look; can you see through my disguise?'

"She looked, and saw her own sad face,
  And trembled, wondering, 'Who art thou?'
'God sent me down to fill your place:
  I am the Virgin Mary now.'

"And with the word, God's mother shone:
  The wanderer whispered, 'Mary, Hail!'
The vision helped her to put on
  Bracelet and fillet, ring and veil.

"'You are sister to the mountains now,
  And sister to the day and night;
Sister to God.' And on the brow
  She kissed her thrice, and left her sight.

"While dreaming in her cloudy bed,
  Far in the crimson orient land,
On many a mountain's happy head
  Dawn lightly laid her rosy hand."

"A Ballad of a Nun" seems to me Mr. Davidson's crowning achievement; yet "A Ballad of Heaven" and "A Ballad of Hell" are scarcely less striking. In "A Ballad of Heaven" there is a musician who works for years at one great composition. The world ignores him. His wife and child, clothed in rags, are starving in their windy garret; but he does not know it, for he dwells in the strange, far heaven of his music.

> " Wistful he grew, but never feared ;
> For always on the midnight skies
> His rich orchestral score appeared,
> In stars and zones and galaxies."

He turns, at last, from his completed score to seek the sympathy of love; but wife and child are lying dead. He gathers to his breast the stark, wan wife with the baby skeleton in her arms.

> " ' You see you are alive,' he cried.
> He rocked them gently to and fro.
> ' No, no, my love, you have not died ;
> Nor you, my little fellow ; no.'

> " Long in his arms he strained his dead,
> And crooned an antique lullaby ;
> Then laid them on the lowly bed,
> And broke down with a doleful cry."

Then his own heart broke, at last, and he, too, was dead.

"Straightway he stood at heaven's gate
  Abashed, and trembling for his sin:
I trow he had not long to wait
  For God came out and led him in.

"And then there ran a radiant pair.
  Ruddy with haste and eager-eyed,
To meet him first upon the stair —
  His wife and child, beatified.

"God, smiling, took him by the hand,
  And led him to the brink of heaven:
He saw where systems whirling stand,
  Where galaxies like snow are driven."

And lo! it was to his own music that the very spheres were moving.

"A Ballad of Hell" tells the story of a woman's love and a woman's courage. Her lover writes her that he must go to prison, unless he marries, the next day, his cousin whom he abhors. There is no refuge but in death; and by her love he conjures her to kill herself at midnight, and meet him, though it must be in Hell. She waited till sleep had fallen on the house. Then out into the night she went, hurried to the trysting oak, and there she drove her dagger home into her heart, and fell on sleep. She woke in Hell. The devil was quite ready to welcome her; but she answered him only —

"'I am young Malespina's bride;
Has he come hither yet?'"

But Malespina had turned coward, when the supreme test came, and he was to marry his cousin on the morrow. For long, and long, she would not believe; but when long waiting brought certainty, at last, she cried —

"'I was betrayed. I will not stay.'"

And straight across the gulf between Hell and Heaven she walked: —

"To her it seemed a meadow fair;
And flowers sprang up about her feet;
She entered Heaven; she climbed the stair,
And knelt down at the mercy-seat."

Next to these three Ballads I should rank "Thirty Bob A Week." It is of the solid earth, and has none of the Dantesque weirdness of the Ballads of Hell and Heaven; but it is stronger than either of them in its own way — this monologue of the man who must live on thirty shillings a week, and make the best of it.

"But the difficultest go to understand,
  And the difficultest job a man can do,
  Is to come it brave and meek, with thirty bob a week,
  And feel that that's the proper thing for you.

"It's a naked child against a hungry wolf;
  It's playing bowls upon a splitting wreck;
  It's walking on a string across a gulf,
  With millstones fore-an-aft about your neck;
  But the thing is daily done by many and many a one;
  And we fall, face-forward, fighting, on the deck."

Here is a man to whom nothing human is foreign — who understands *because* he feels.

It is the "Ballads" rather than the "Songs," which give to this book its exceptional value, yet some of the Songs are charming — for instance, the two "To the Street Piano," "A Laborer's Wife," and "After the End." Indeed there is nothing in the volume more deeply imbued with the human sympathy, of which Mr. Davidson's work is so pregnant, than these two songs. Witness the refrain to the one which the laborer's wife sings : —

> "Oh! once I had my fling!
> I romped at ging-go-ring;
> I used to dance and sing,
> And play at everything.
> I never feared the light;
> I shrank from no one's sight;
> I saw the world was right;
> I always slept at night."

But in an evil hour she married, "on the sly." Now three pale children fight and whine all day; her "man" gets drunk; her head and her bones are sore; and her heart is hacked; and she sings —

> "Now I fear the light;
> I shrink from every sight;
> I see there's nothing right;
> I hope to die to-night."

"After the End" is in a very different key. It is more universal. Kings and queens, as well as the humblest of their subjects, may well cry out, into the unknown dark —

> "After the end of all things,
> After the years are spent,
> After the loom is broken,
> After the robe is rent,

The Man Who Dares

Will there be hearts a-beating,
Will friend converse with friend,
Will men and women be lovers,
After the end?"

"In Romney Marsh" is a fascinating bit of landscape-painting; and "A Cinque Port" has a melancholy and suggestive beauty that makes me long for space to copy it. The "Songs" for "Spring," "Summer," "Autumn," and "Winter" are charming, also.

There is thought enough and strength enough in the "Songs," "To the New Women," and "To the New Men;" but they are rhymed prose, rather than poetry — if, indeed, "what" and "hot" can be said to *rhyme* with "thought."

Why, oh why, does Mr. Davidson treat us to such uncouth words as "bellettrist," and "moneyers," and "strappadoes"? — why talk to us of "apes in lusts unspoken," and "fools, who lick the lip and roll the lustful eye"? "The Exodus From Houndsditch," which contains these phrases, is certainly hard reading; but one is compelled, all the same, to read it more than once, for it is pregnant with thought, and here and there it is starred with splendid lines, such as —

By Louise Chandler Moulton

" The chill wind whispered winter; night set in;
  Stars flickered high; and like a tidal wave,
  He heard the rolling multitudinous din
  Of life the city lave — "

or the picture of some fantastic world,

" Where wild weeds half way down the frowning bank
  Flutter, like poor apparel stained and sere,
  And lamplight flowers, with hearts of gold, their rank
  And baleful blossoms rear."

One closes Mr. Davidson's book with reluctance, and with a haunting sense of beauty, and power, and the promise of yet greater things to come. He is a young man — scarcely past thirty; what laurels are springing up for him to gather in the future, who shall say? Happily he is not faultless — since for the faultless there is no perspective of hope.

R. L. S. — Some Edinburgh Notes

By
Eve Blantyre Simpson

R. L. S.—SOME EDINBURGH NOTES

> Give me again all that was there,
> Give me the sun that shone!
> Give me the eyes, give me the soul,
> Give me the lad that's gone!
> ROBERT LOUIS STEVENSON.

LOUIS STEVENSON was born in 8 Howard Place, then an outlying suburban street between Edinburgh and the sea; and the substantial but unpretending house with its small plot of garden in front will doubtless be visited with interest in future by those who like to look on the birthplaces of famous men.

17 Heriot Row, on one of Edinburgh's level terraces between the steep hills, "from which you see a perspective of a mile or so of falling street," became his home before he was out of velvet tunics and socks, but as his mother was delicate, they lived when the weather was genial " in the green lap of the Rutland Hills," at Swanston, a few miles from Edin-

burgh. He, however, spent his winters at Heriot Row, when he grew into an Academy boy, though not a specially brilliant scholar. His doubtful health would often stand as an excuse, when the rain splattered on the panes, or the square gardens opposite were hid in a scowling "haur," for the small Louis to remain and "Child Play" beside his pretty mother. No doubt, too, the truant spirit was strong within him when he trotted down hill to school, "rasping his clachan[1] on the area railings" as he made an Edinburgh hero of his do. We first knew Louis Stevenson when his schooldays and teens were past, and he was facing what he called "the equinoctial gales of youth," and beginning to put his self-taught art of writing into print. He had great railings against his native town in these days, which were somewhere in the heart of the seventies. The "meteorological purgatory" of its climate embittered him, as his frail frame suffered sorely from the bleak blasts. He vowed his fellow-townsmen had a list to one side by reason of having to struggle against the East wind. He gave his spleen vent in "Pictur-

[1] A clachan is a wooden racket Edinburgh Academy boys play ball with.

esque Notes of Edinburgh," yet by way of apology he says, "the place establishes an interest in people's hearts; go where they will, they find no city of the same distinction, go where they will, they take a pride in their old home." No one could clothe the historical tales of Edinburgh in more graphic words than this slim son of hers. Often he would talk thereon, and he speaks of his joy, as a lad, in finding "a nugget of cottages at Broughton;" and any bit of old village embedded in the modern town, he espied and rejoiced over. He would frequently drop in to dinner with us, and of an evening he had the run of our smoking-room. After 10 P. M., when a stern old servant went to bed, the "open sesame" to our door was a rattle on the letter-box. He liked this admittance by secret sign, and we liked to hear his special rat-a-tat, for we knew we would then enjoy an hour or two of talk which, he said, "is the harmonious speech of two or more, and is by far the most accessible of pleasures." He always adhered to the same dress for all entertainments, a shabby, short, velveteen jacket, a loose, Byronic, collared shirt (for a brief space he adopted black flannel ones), and meagre, shabby-looking trousers. His straight hair he wore long, and he looked like an unsuccessful artist, or a poorly-clad but eager student. He was then fragile in figure and, to use a Scottish expression, *shilpit* looking. There is no English equivalent for *shilpit*, being lean, starveling, ill-thriven, in one. His dark, bright eyes were his most noticeable and attractive feature, — wide apart, almost Japanese in their shape, and above them a fine brow.

He was pale and sallow, and there was a foreign, almost gypsy look about him, despite his long-headed Scotch ancestry. In the "Inland Voyage," he complains, he "never succeeded in persuading a single official abroad of his nationality." I do not wonder he was suspected of being a spy with false passports, for he had a very un-British smack about him; but, slim and pinched-looking though he was, he still commanded notice by his unique appearance and his vivacity of expression. His manners, too, had a foreign air with waving gestures, elaborate bows, and a graceful nimbleness of action.

By our library fire, on the winter evenings, he planned the canoe trip with my brother, and told us in the following season how the record of this "Inland Voyage" progressed. He was also laying future plans for a further trip, as he said, smiling with fun, with another donkey,—this time to the Cevennes. After the "Inland Voyage," Louis was full of a project to buy a barge and saunter through the canals of Europe, Venice being the far-off terminus. A few select shareholders in this scheme were chosen, mostly artists, for the barge plan was projected in the mellow autumnal days at Fontainebleau Forest where artists abounded. Robert A. Stevenson, Louis's cousin, then a wielder of the brush, was to be of the company. He, too, though he came of the shrewd Scottish civil engineer stock, had, like his kinsman, a foreign look and a strong touch of Bohemianism in him. He, also, with these alien looks, had his cousin's attractive power of speech and fertile imagination. The barge company were then all in the hey-day of their youth. They were to paint fame-enduring pictures, as they leisurely sailed through life and Europe, and when bowed, gray-bearded, bald-headed men, they were to cease their journeyings at Venice. There, before St. Marks, a crowd of clamorously eager picture-dealers and lovers of art were to be waiting to purchase the wonderful work of the wanderers. The scene in the piazza of St. Marks on the barge's arrival, and the excited throng of anxious buyers, the hoary-headed artists, tottering under the weight of canvases, was pictured in glowing colors by their author, when the forest was smelling of the "ripe breath of autumn." The barge was purchased, but bankruptcy presently stared its shareholders in the face. The picture-dealers of that day were not thirsting to buy shareholders' pictures. The man of the pen had only ventured on an "Inland Voyage," and as yet no golden harvest for his work lined the pockets of his velveteen coat. The barge was arrested and, with it, the canoes which have earned an everlasting fame through the "Arethusa's" pen. They were rescued, the barge sold, and the company wound up.

We saw most of Louis Stevenson in winter, when studies and rough weather held him in Edinburgh. In summer he was off to the country, abroad, or yachting on the West coast, for in his posthumous song he truly says: —

"Merry of soul he sailed on a day
Over the sea to Skye."

As a talker by the winter's fireside in these unknown-to-fame days, we give him the crown for being the king of speakers. His reading, his thoughts thereon, his plans, he described with a graphic and nimble tongue, accompanied by the queer, flourishing gesticulations and the "speaking gestures" of his thin, sensitive hands. We teased him unmercifully for his peculiarities in dress and manner. It did not become a youth of his years, we held, to affect a bizarre style, and he held he lived in a free country, and could exercise his own taste at will. Nothing annoyed him more than to affirm his shabby clothes, his long cloak, which he wore instead of an orthodox great-coat, were eccentricities of genius. He certainly liked to be noticed, for he was full of the self-absorbed conceit of youth. If he was not the central figure, he took what we called Stevensonian ways of attracting notice to himself. He would spring up full of a novel notion he had to expound (and his brain teemed with them), or he vowed he could not speak trammelled by a coat, and asked leave to talk in his shirt-sleeves. For all these mannerisms he had to stand a good deal of chaff, which he never resented, though he vehemently defended himself or fell squashed for a brief space in a limp mass into a veritable back seat.

R. S. L. — Some Edinburgh Notes

Looking back through the mellowing vista of years these little eccentric whims were all very harmless and guileless, and I own we were hard on the susceptible lad, but, as we told him, it was for his good, and if he had been like ourselves, with a band of brothers, egotisms would have been stamped out in the nursery. He would, after a severe shower of chaff, put out his cigarette, wind himself in his cloak and silently, with an elaborate bow, go off; but, to his credit be it said, he bore no ill-will. His very sensitiveness was to his tormentors conceit. He wrote of himself later that he was "a very humble-minded youth, though it was a virtue he never had much credit for." He is credited now with it, for as the then "uncharted desert of the future" lies mapped out, we see that his fantastic ways were not affectations, but second nature, to which the life he chose in the subtle south was an appropriate setting. We never, though we gibed him sorely, found fault with his enthusiasm; it was so infectious and refreshing. He was always brimful of new ideas, new ventures, full of sweeping changes, a rabid radical, a religious doubter; though with him, as with many others, there was more "belief in honest doubt than half their creeds." He had an almost child-like fund of insatiable curiosity. He thirsted to know how it would feel to be in other people's shoes, from those of a king to a beggar, and he smoked on the hearth rug an endless succession of cigarettes and put his imaginations thereof into words.

He was very sore and somewhat rebellious over writing not being considered a profession, and having to bend to his good father in so far as to join the Scottish bar. For long "R. L. Stevenson, Advocate," was on the door-plate of 17 Heriot Row. The Parliament House saw him seldom, never therein to practise his bewigged profession. We frightened him much by avowing that a clerk was hunting for him, and even the rich library below the trampling advocate's feet could not wile him into the old Hall for some time after that false scare. He also heard he had been dubbed "That Gifted Boy and the New Chatterton" by an idle legal wit. That name more nearly persuaded him to have his hair shorn to an orthodox length than any other entreaty. Like all people with character, he had animosities, but he was very just and tolerant in belaboring an adversary with his tongue, which, considering he was in the full bloom of the critical self-satisfiedness of youth, showed a just mind and kindliness of heart. When he had fallen foul of and had hurled some sarcasms at the stupid dulness of people, he next, in his queer inquisitive way, fell to wondering what it would be like to be inside their torpid minds and view things from their dead level. He was fond of travel, of boating, of walking tours, but he was no sportsman, and not even a lover of the Gentle Art. Though his friends were all golfers (and golf then was mostly confined to Scotland), I do not think he ever took a club in hand. His eyes, when outside, were wholly occupied enjoying his surroundings and painting them in words. "Even in the thickest of our streets," he noted, "the country hill-tops find out a young man's eyes and set his heart beating for travel and pure air." He loved to wander round his native city. Duddingstone was one favorite haunt, Queensferry was another, and the Hawes Inn there, now grown into a villafied hotel, with the hawthorn hedges still in its garden, had attractions for him. From it Davie Balfour was "kidnapped," and Rest-

By Eve Blantyre Simpson

And-Be-Thankful on Corstorphine Hill, where Allan and Davie part after their adventures, we often walked to on Sundays, and all the while he was busy talking and full of plans and projects. The Jekyll and Hyde plot he had in his brain, and told us of in those days. Burke and Hare had a fascination for him. A novel called the " Great North Road " was another plot in his mind. His " Virginibus Puerisque " is dedicated to W. E. Henley, of whom I heard Stevenson speak when he had first discovered him an invalid in the Edinburgh Infirmary. He came in glowing with delight at the genius he had found and began ransacking our shelves for books for him. A few days later he was bristling with indignation because some people who visited the sick objected to the advanced and foreign literary food Stevenson had fed his new acquaintance on, and left a new supply of tract literature in their stead. In the preface of " Virginibus Puerisque," which is dedicated to Mr. Henley, Stevenson says : " These papers are like milestones on the wayside of my life." To those who knew him in these past days to re-read these papers seem to travel the same road again in the same good company. They recall the slight, boyish-looking youth they knew, and to those who live under the stars which Stevenson thought shone so bright — the Edinburgh street lamps — he was not so much the famous author, as the sympathetic comrade, the unique, ideal talker we welcomed of yore. As he truly said, "The powers and the ground of friendship are a mystery," but looking back I can discern in part we loved the thing he was, for some shadow of what he was to be.

Mr. Gilbert Parker's Sonnets

By
Richard Henry Stoddard

MR. GILBERT PARKER'S SONNETS.[1]

A SEQUENCE of songs, of which this collection of Mr. Parker's sonnets is an example, is more recondite and remote than most of its readers probably imagine. It would be as difficult to trace its origins as to trace springs, which, flowing from many subterranean sources, unite somewhere in one current, and force their way onward and upward until they appear at last, and are hailed as the well-heads of famous rivers. Who will may trace its beginnings to the lays of the troubadours, which were nothing if they were not amorous: I am content to find them on Italian soil in the sonnets of Petrarch, and on English soil in the sonnets of Wyatt and Surrey. What the literatures of Greece and Rome were to men of letters the world over, once they were freed from the seclusion of the manuscripts which sheltered them so long, the literature of Italy was to English

---

[1] "A Lover's Diary. Songs in Sequence." By Gilbert Parker. Cambridge and Chicago: Stone & Kimball. MDCCCXCIV. London: Methuen & Co.

men of letters from the days of Chaucer down. They read Italian more than they read Latin and Greek: they wrote Italian, not more clumsily, let us hope, than they wrote English: and they sojourned in Italy, if they could get there, not greatly to their spiritual welfare, if the satirists of their time are to be believed. One need not be deeply read in English literature of the sixteenth century to perceive its obligations to Italian literature, to detect the influences of Boccaccio, and Bandello, and other Italian story-tellers in its drama, and the influence of Italian poets in its poetry, particularly the influence of Petrarch, the sweetness, the grace, the ingenuity of whose amorous effusions captivated the facile nature of so many English singers. He was the master of Wyatt and Surrey, who, tracking their way through the snow of his footprints, introduced the sonnet form into English verse, and, so far as they might, the sonnet spirit, as they understood it. They allowed themselves, however, licenses of variation in the construction of their octaves and sextets, which, judging from his avoidance of them, would have displeased Petrarch, — a proceeding which was followed by their immediate successors, who seldom observed the strict laws of the Petrarchian sonnet. Whether the sonnets of Wyatt and Surrey were expressions of genuine emotion, or were merely poetic exercises, is not evident in the sonnets themselves, which are formal and frigid productions. They were handed round in manuscript copies, and greatly admired in the courtly circles in which their authors moved, and ten years after the death of Surrey were collected by Master Richard Tottell, to whom belongs the honor of publishing the first miscellany of English verse. That this miscellany, the original title of which was "Songs and Sonnets written by the ryght honorable Lorde Henry Howard, late Earle of Surrey and other," was very popular is certain from the number of editions through which it passed, and from the number of similar publications by which it was followed. It was an epoch-making book, like the "Reliques" of good Bishop Percy two centuries afterwards, and like that rare miscellany was fruitful of results in the direction of what chiefly predominated there, — the current of personal expression in amatory sonnets. The first notable scholar of Wyatt and Surrey, a scholar who surpassed his masters in every poetical quality, was

Mr. Gilbert Parker's Sonnets

Sir Philip Sidney, whose sequence of sonnets was given to the world five years after his death as "Astrophel and Stella." This was in 1591. Samuel Daniel appeared the next year with a sequence entitled "Delia," Michael Drayton a year later with a sequence entitled "Idea," and two years after that came Edmund Spenser with a sequence entitled "Amoretti." The frequency of the sonnet form in English verse was determined at this time by this cluster of poets, to which the names of Constable, Griffin, and others might be added, and determined for all time by their great contemporary, whose proficiency as a sonneteer, outside of his comedies, was chiefly confined to the knowledge of "Mr. W. H." and his friends until 1609. To what extent this treasury of sonnets is read now I have no means of knowing; but it cannot, I think, be a large one, the fashion of verse has changed so much since they were written. They should be read for what they are rather than what we might wish them to be; in other words, from the Elizabethan and not the Victorian point of view. So read they seem to me "choicely good," as Walton said of their like, though I cannot say that they are much better than the strong lines that are now in fashion in this critical age. Only two of these sonnet sequences are known to have been inspired by real persons, Sidney's "Astrophel and Stella," which celebrates his enamourment of Lady Rich, and consists of one hundred and eight sonnets and eleven songs, and Spenser's "Amoretti," which celebrates his admiration for the unknown beauty whom he married during his residence in Ireland, and which consists of eighty-eight sonnets, and an epithalamium. Of the two sequences, the Sidneyan is the more poetical, and making allowance for the artificial manner in which it is written, the more impassioned, certain of the sonnets authenticating their right to be considered genuine by virtue of their qualities as portraiture, their self-betrayal of the character of Sidney, and the vividness of their picturesque descriptions or suggestions. Such I conceive to be the twenty-seventh ("Because I oft, in dark, abstracted guise"), the thirty-first ("With how sad steps, O moon, thou climb'st the skies"), the forty-first ("Having this day my horse, my hand, my lance"), the fifty-fourth ("Because I breathe not love to every one"), the eighty-fourth ("Highway, since you my chief Parnassus be"), and the one hundred and third ("O happy Thames, that didst my Stella bear"). If Sidney had followed the advice of his Muse in the first of these sonnets,

"Fool, said my Muse to me, look in thy heart and write,"

that noble heart would surely have taught him to write in a simpler and more sincere fashion than he permitted himself to do in "Astrophel and Stella," which is more important for what it promised than for what it achieved.

The ease of a more practised poet than Sidney lived to be is manifest in Spenser's "Amoretti,"—as manifest there, I think, as in "The Faerie Queene," the musical cadences of whose stanzas and, to a certain extent, its rhythmical construction are translated into sonnetry; but, taken as a whole, they are as hard reading as most easy writing. They are fluent and diffuse, but devoid of felicities of expression, and the note of distinction which Sidney sometimes attains. Daniel and Drayton were reckoned excellent poets by their contemporaries, and measured by their standards, and within their limitations, they were; but their excellence did not embrace the emotion which the writing of amatory sonnets demands, nor the art of simulating it successfully, for the "Delia" of the one was as surely an ideal mistress as the "Idea" of the other. The substance of Drayton's sonnets is more prosaic than that of Daniel's and his touch is less felicitous, is so infelicitous, in fact, that only one of the sixty-three of which the sequence is composed lingers in the memory as the expression of what may have been genuine feeling. The sonnets of Daniel are distinguished for sweetness of versification, for graces of expression, and for a vein of tender and pensive thought which was native to him. One of them (there are fifty-seven in all) which begins, "Care-charmer Sleep, son of the sable night," recalls a similar invocation to sleep in "Astrophel and Stella," and others, especially the nineteenth, which begins, "Restore thy tresses to the golden ore," remind us of some of the sonnets of Shakespeare, whose first master in sonnetry was as certainly Samuel Daniel, as in dramatic writing Christopher Marlowe.

Of the sonnets of Shakespeare, I shall say nothing here, for though they form a sequence, the sequence is not of the kind which the sonnets of Sidney and Daniel and Drayton and Spenser illustrate, and of which the purpose is to celebrate the love of a man for a woman, but of a kind which the genius of Shakespeare originated, and which deals with the friendship of a man and for a man, and of which the most noteworthy example is Tennyson's "In Memoriam." I pass, therefore, from Spenser to Drummond of Hawthornden, who, in the year of Shakespeare's death, published in his second collection of verse a series of sonnets, songs, sextains, and madrigals, the majority of which are of an amatory nature. Modelled after the manner of his Italian and English predecessors, and consequently academical rather than individual, they are characterized by tenderness of sentiment and a vein of melancholy reflection, by studied graces of scholarly phrasing which are not free from Scotticisms, and by a chastened remembrance of his sorrow for the loss of Mary Cunningham, the daughter of a laird, who was carried off by a fever before the arrival of their nuptial day. The line of amatory sonneteers ended with Drummond; but not the line of amatory poets, the best of whom (apart from mere lyrists like Lovelace and Suckling) was William Habington, who in 1634–1635 celebrated his affection for Lucia, daughter of William,

Lord Powis, and the worst of whom was Abraham Cowley, who, at a later period, celebrated nobody in "The Mistress, or Several Copies of Love-Verses." There are exquisite things in "Castara," the title of which is fully justified by the spiritual purity of the love of which it is a memorial, and there are execrable things in "The Mistress," where the fancy of Cowley exhausted itself in a profusion of ingenious conceits, the brilliant absurdity of which is absolutely bewildering. Love there is none, nor any serious pretence of it, Cowley's motive in writing being that poets are scarce thought free-men of their Company, without paying some duties, and obliging themselves to be true to Love.

To follow the succession of English amatory poets later than their founders, the writers of sonnet sequences and their lyrical children, lies outside the purpose of this paper, which is simply to trace the position of Mr. Parker; so I shall say nothing of two illustrious and comparatively recent members of the guild, one being Mr. Dante Gabriel Rossetti, who in "The House of Life" has preserved and Italianated the romantic traditions of Sidney and Daniel, and the other, Mrs. Elizabeth Barrett Browning, whose "Sonnets from the Portuguese" are the most impassioned utterances of love in any language, linking her name forever with the burning name of Sappho. I find in "A Lover's Diary" a quality which is not common in the verse of to-day, and which I find nowhere in its fulness except in the poetry of the age of Elizabeth. To describe what evades description, I should call it suggestion,—a vague hinting at rather than a distinct exposition of feeling and thought, — the prescience of things which never beheld are always expected, the remembrance of things which are only known through the shadows they leave behind them, the perception of uncommon capacities for pain, the anticipation of endless energies for pleasure, the instinctive discovery and enjoyment of the secret inspirations of love. The method which Mr. Parker preserves is that of the early masters, whose sole business when they wrote sonnets was to write sonnets, not caring what they proved, or whether they proved anything, not disdaining logic, though not solicitous to obey its laws, not avid for nor averse from the use of imagery; content, in the best words they had, to free their minds of what was in them. They wrote well or ill, according to their themes and moods, but nobly, gloriously, when at their best; and to be reminded of them by a sonneteer of to-day, as I am by Mr. Parker, is a poetic enjoyment which is not often vouchsafed to me.

Is the New Woman New?
By
Maurice Thompson

IS THE NEW WOMAN NEW?

(VARIUM ET MUTABILE SEMPER FEMINA)

IT is impossible to resist the New Woman, mainly, perhaps, on account of her moral fascination; but somewhat is due in this behalf to a certain perspective which, reaching into the enchantment of remote times, connects her with a picturesque succession of New Women.

The question might be raised to decide, even at this late hour, between Eve and Lilith; which of them was the progressive, representative female?

There have been notable personages, all along the line of the centuries, who have added grace or disgrace to their sex by vigorous assertion of new-womanhood. From the Hebrew woman who drove the nail into her enemy's head, along down by way of the Greek philosopher's wife, to Queen Elizabeth, as thoroughly authentic records seem to establish, an unbroken strain of man-harrying amazons march through history. And side by side with it another procession is composed of the intellectual prodigies of various female types who have assaulted the masculine stronghold of science and art, from the days of Sappho to this good hour.

Charles Baudelaire, in one of his "Fleurs du Mal," longs for the day of giantesses, and tuning his harp to the major key of desire, sings with superb gallantry to the beat of an enormous plectrum : —

"Du temps que la Nature en sa verve puissante
  Concevait chaque jour des enfants monstrueux
  J'eusse aimé vivre auprès d'une jeune géante,
  Comme aux pieds d'une reine un chat voluptueux."

Of course a poet is sure to use strong language which goes better with some grains of salt; but there is no doubt touching the following sketch of a New Woman : —

"J'eusse aimé   .   .   .   .   .   .
  Ramper sur le versant de ses genoux énormes,
  Et parfois en été, quand les soleils malsains,
  Lasse, la font s'étendre à travers la campagne,
  Dormir nonchalamment à l'ombre de ses seins,
  Comme un hameau paisible au pied d'une montagne."

To be a very large woman's little cat might not satisfy the highest aspiration of a manly man, even among *fin de siècle* poets; and to be as a mere village in her bosom's mountain shadow is not open to consideration in the most degenerate masculine mind of our epoch. Still Baudelaire's verses, being neither humor nor satire, adumbrate a possible outcome of civilization, were the New Woman to take a giant-esque turn. She might be supremely pleased with having man purring at her toes, or hopelessly asleep in her shadow.

Some uneasiness on the subject undoubtedly exists in certain male imaginations. Not long ago I said to a friend of mine that I was willing for women to vote on equal terms with men; that I considered their enfranchisement a matter for them to settle; if they in committee of the whole should declare for this thing, let them have it as a matter of course. My friend bridled. "Yes, let them have it," he cried; "let them run the government woman-fashion for a while. There's no danger in the experiment. When we get tired of them, we can take empty guns and scare them quite out of the country. Indeed it would be fun."

To avoid a hot political discussion I fell into his humor and suggested that the New Woman was waxing athletic; that her muscles were changing;

she was even beginning to throw a stone by the true arm-wheel motion, as boys and men do. And I drew his attention to the young ladies on bicycles gliding past. Then there were the fencing schools, too, and the woman's shooting galleries, where girls were taught military doings. What did he imagine might come of permitting this progress toward physical equality? Mayhap, on some dire day, a second Jeanne d'Arc would call to the New Woman, as did the other to chivalric man, and lead the way to wonders of conquest, instead of being scared by empty guns.

"Jeanne d'Arc was, indeed, a typical New Woman," he snarled; "she led on to Rouen." He pronounced it *ruin*. "And you will please remember her successor at Lyons." This was his Parthian arrow; he shot it back over his shoulder, in hasty retreat meantime, and it stuck and rankled in my critical curiosity. I cudgelled memory to recollect who could be this *lyonnaise* so tantalizingly enmisted in allusion; one is not to be censured for being taken aback; Lyons is a small city, little but old, and a long ways off; moreover mine adversary had left me no date.

CHAP-BOOK ESSAYS

By Maurice Thompson

You can trust a provincial, however, when it comes to a matter of provincial history. A short day's rummaging served my turn. Louise Labé presented herself to me in a new light, a striking figure seen through three and a third centuries of feminine aspiration, struggle, and change. As in the case of Sappho, the woman was beset by coarse defamers, men who made a sort of middle comedies at her expense, and doubtless she behaved measurably in accordance with the social influences of her time and place; but she was a New Woman, notably independent, original, and strong.

During the course of a fascinating study in which I reviewed everything at hand having relation to the life of this remarkable and much maligned woman, the world-old attitude of the Literary Libertine was projected afresh. The man who, in the name of gallantry, writes shame on the record of beauty, genius, and strength, merely because they chance to be the possession of a woman, stood before me in full stature.

Louise Labé, known as *La Belle Cordière*, was born at Lyons in the year 1526. Her real name, before her marriage with Ennemond Perrin, was probably Charlin; but she wrote over the signature of Louise Labé, and her poetry immortalized it. I do not feel like recommending any of her writings. They are historically and artistically interesting; but one finds them out-paganing the pagans in some most objectionable essentials. What attracts me in her behalf is a certain rudimentary foresay uttered by her, not so much in her literature as through her life, a foresay comprehending the modern feminine aspiration. Nor would I be understood to mean that I admire her attitude or her aim; many qualifications would be necessary; but she is attractive because she is a significant figure.

Her father was a *cordier*, or a ship-supply merchant, or both; at all events, he was rich and gave his daughter a most liberal education. Lyons at that time was a literary centre, one of those spots in the south of France made intellectually fertile by the residuary influence of Italian and Spanish residents of earlier days. Like Avignon, it was a singing station on the bank of the melodious Rhone, contributing its odes and ballads and chansons to the medley which went gayly on down through the hills to the Mediterranean at Les Bouches.

CHAP-BOOK ESSAYS

By Maurice Thompson

When Louise was sixteen, that is to say in the year 1542, Francis I. laid siege to Perpignan, which precisely a hundred years later became permanently a city of France. The siege was a dismal failure; but some daring deeds were done in its behalf. For hard fighting and distinguished personal valor honored those dying days of old chivalry. A striking figure, a youthful Captain Loys, all armored and lance-bearing, came into view at Perpignan.

This was Louise Labé, in her rôle of New Woman, an apparition sure to storm the hearts of men if not the salients of Perpignan. As she herself sings, she was seen —

> " En armes fière aller,
> Porter la lance et bois faire aller,
> Le devoir faire en l'estour furieux,
> Piquer, volter le cheval glorieux."

Cervantes might sneer in vain at this rich new bloom of knighthood. What would Sidney or Bayard have counted for at sixteen beside her in the burning imagination of the Midi? One of our American poets, a woman who sings of divine right, truly says —

> " There is no sex in courage and in pain."

Is the New Woman New?

Louise Labé had courage of the first order. Helmet and breastplate, steel boot and clinking spur decorated an embodied defiance when she rode down to the beleaguered stronghold. Captain Loys represented a revolt of girlhood against the sugar-coated sex-slavery of the times.

My cynical friend had some good ground for citing *La Belle Cordière* as an example of disaster. Her campaign came to nothing; she returned to Lyons, married a rich rope-man, and went into the business of writing erotic verse. But why do so many women, and over and over again, commit this blighting mistake in the course of their battle for liberty? Must the New Woman inevitably get herself entangled in the meshes of the illicit? I think not. Good mothers, faithful wives, and healthy-minded sweethearts are not to be crowded out of the army of progress and reform; they are in to stay; but the Louise Labés are also a persistent element, and unfortunately the noisiest and apparently most influential, especially in the field of literature.

Woman must come to her own; she must have full freedom; would that to-morrow were the day of it; but not if she is to be like the wife in the

CHAP-BOOK ESSAYS
By Maurice Thompson

"Heavenly Twins," not if she must take pattern by a "Yellow Aster" heroine, a "Key-Notes" woman, a "Daughter of Music," or any of the still worse models set up by the latest female propagandists of social and domestic reform. These writers of polemical fiction favoring the new order of social license are at present more in evidence than the rest of them. Man, brutal Man, would be quite justified in appealing to his superior muscle to prevent the arrival of this New Woman, or to hale her to prison, as an enemy of the race, should she prove clever enough to break through the masculine guard. One laughs, nevertheless, thinking how justly and effectively these decadent women might retort by wondering what manner of government and civilization we should have were the Tolstois, the Hardys, the Maupassants, the George Moores, the Zolas, the Ibsens, and the Hall Caines given the law-making and law-executing powers! A beautiful suggestion. I can think of no political absurdity so deep, no domestic calamity so comprehensively terrible. Perhaps our bluff American senator was inspired when he objected to "them literary fellers" being recognized as political possibilities, and I can fully realize the untainted unction with which the English judge sent a certain be-sunflowered æsthete to hard prison labor upon a recent occasion. The general principle is that an unsexed woman and an emasculate man ought to be considered as outlaws.

When Captain Loys rode down to Perpignan on her glorious war-horse, she doubtless sang many an amazonian battle-song foretasting from afar the triumph of the New Woman when she should mount to the bastion coping and fling out the banner of France. Some months later, riding homeward up the fertile valley of the Rhone, she changed her tune to a plaintive, backward-going wail for a lost lover who had proved untrue. Farewell to Roussillon, to dreams of military glory, to all the fierce throbs of war — and good-by to the stalwart, fickle soldier who broke her heart!

It is Captain Loys no longer; the lance lies back yonder somewhere under the curtain of Perpignan's fort; the helmet is too heavy; the steel boots have tired the dainty feet, and the embossed shield is gone from the girl's left arm. Pretty Louise Labé sits sidewise on a palfrey pacing gently up to Lyons; she is going home to marry, forlorn and loveless, an easy-going and rich *cordier* with a luxurious home and a garden by the Rhone. The New Woman has tried to be a man, and a man has, by the ancient test, shown her the folly of it.

To a lusty youth a thing of that sort is filliped aside and forgotten; the girl lays it deep in her heart. He and she have met; he goes on his way whistling a troubadour catch, she loses faith in every soul under heaven; and likely enough the worst that passed between them was a tender word or two, possibly a kiss. You see God built us for different tasks; and the true New Woman knows it; she would like to be rid of the Labés. Yet somehow these Yellow Book Girls make all the noise, lead the van and get most of the attention.

"There is our weak point," said a noble woman to me; she is one of the fine, strong spirits in the work of lifting her sex to true freedom; "there is our chief obstacle. The divorced women, or 'grass widows,' the drunkards' wives, and the disappointed old maids, are assuming leadership, taking it by vulgar force. This sets the men against us and gives them that irresistible weapon, ridicule. The women we most need for leaders and followers are the happy wives and mothers. We want the women who have not lost faith in men, marriage, and maternity, the three great M's. Not that we have no sympathy with our unfortunate and unhappy sisters; but the woman with a grievance, a moan of woe in her throat, and a score to settle with Fate, is not a vote-maker. She irritates the men, and they tell her that she should have had better luck. She seems to forget that it is from the men that our boom must come, and that they will never grant it while our dyspeptics are to the fore. Who, indeed, cares a straw for what an unsuccessful person screams to possess?"

Now, this good woman may have been too hard upon the class she was talking at, I dare say she was; but there was excellent political wisdom in her words. The Louise Labés are naturally somewhat jaundiced and hysterical; when the adventures of Captain Loys are over the next thing is a career against Fate and the limits of sex. But it is to those who already have plenty and to spare that fortune tumbles down her largest gifts, not to the empty-handed and greedy-eyed failures who have nothing but a song of dole to sing.

CHAP-BOOK ESSAYS

By Maurice Thompson

Louise Labé went the common road of the irresponsible New Woman in literature, the road so very popular to-day, which is paved with erotic poetry and the fiction of free love and marital infidelity, beginning her new life by posing as a victim bound in loveless marriage-chains on the altar of monstrous social injustice. Her poetry was super-Sapphic and addressed to the other man, not her husband, a man who presumably was above the trade of a *cordier,* and therefore irresistible to the low-born poetess.

We must distinctly agree with Sainte-Beuve, who chivalrously acquits Louise Labé of actual personal dishonor. This thing of dressing up a literary effigy and labelling it with the lyrical egotism as self-expression is an old poetic ruse, a fiction of the Muses. Louise was good enough for her time and place. She imagined herself a sociologist, and somehow got it in mind that the only purpose of sociology is by hook or crook to get rid of the sanctity of the marriage relation. Indeed, if we may judge the New Woman, from Louise's time to now, by her poems and fictions, we must inevitably conclude that she would define sociology as the science of making the social evil appear harmlessly attractive;

or that, like some of our contemporaries, she would travel all the way to Russia to get the pattern of Tolstoi's trousers, having in mind a stunning new bicycle suit, or a lecture upon dress-reform. She is not humorous; but she makes a good deal of fun for the men.

After all it may be that the New Woman is a recurring decimal, as the arithmeticians would say, appearing at certain intervals with a constantly shifting value to civilization. If she persists in being rather ornamental than useful, taken as a noun of multitude, we are all the more her debtor on the side of romance, which —

"Loves to nod and sing,"

and which, if it cannot always get "sweetness and light" to charm itself withal, gladly accepts sweetness and chic instead. Half way between a grotesque gargoyle and a dainty flower-ornament of our social and domestic structure, there is, perhaps, a mean at which the New Woman is aiming; at all events she means to be decorative, as she always has been, and down the ages ahead of us she will doubtless continue to charm, amuse, and marry man, proving herself to him a great luxury, but notably expensive.

The Return of the Girl
By
Maurice Thompson

THE RETURN OF THE GIRL

> τάδε νῦν ἑταίραις
> ταῖς ἔμαισι τέρπνα καλῶς ἀείσω.
> — SAPPHO, *Frag. II.*

TO begin with, a girl is, generally speaking, an interesting organism, and a perfect specimen finds prompt welcome in any cabinet. The type is not paleozoic; at all events no fossil remains have yet been discovered in any of the rocks; but Jane Austen may serve in that stead, duly pinned and labelled archeparthenos.

Not of grizzled spinsters dully staring, in the mummy stage of existence, out of vitreous eyes furnished by the taxidermist, but of plump, sound, hearty young girls do we now wish some scientific notes. Let the withered type-specimens remain in their glass cases for the benefit of Professor Shelfdust and the English novelists: our heroine is yet under twenty years of age; she has never heard of sociology and is marvellously ignorant of the ethics of elopement; but she is as clever as she is fascinating.

Sappho knew the value of her sex in the bud, when perfect girl nature was just beginning to let go its charming essentials upon the air.

"τίς δ' ἀγροιῶτίς τοι θέλγει νόον
οὐκ ἐπισταμένα τὰ βράκε' ἔγκην ἐπὶ τῶν σφύρων;"

"What rustic lass can win your heart
Without a touch of girlish art?"

Or literally: "What rustic maiden, even, can captivate your mind, if she is not clever at drawing her skirts around her ankles?" There shows the brush of genius, a fine stroke, like the circle of Giotto, projecting a complete figure; and it is warm with life. The girl is pretty, brown as a berry, smiling, and lissomely graceful. Her sophistication is altogether hereditary. Sidney had her in mind when he wrote:—

"Gay hair, more gay than straw when harvest lies,
Lips red and plump as cherries' ruddy side,
Eyes fair and great, like fair great ox's eyes, . . .
. . . Flesh as soft as wool new dressed,
And yet as hard as brawn made hard by art."

Like a bird in a bush, the strong, healthy girl shows her decorations with enthusiastic willingness, yet shyly, flitting betimes and keeping quite out of reach, while apparently not thinking of danger. Even the wild lass, saucing Daphnis from the doorway of her cave, knew perfectly well that he would hang his head and pass by. She was σύνοφρυς κόρα; that is, her eyebrows ran together across her nose, which was not as unfortunate as Herrick's sort of girl, who was —

> "One of those
> That an acre hath of nose."

Why will the thought of berries come up? Dear old Suckling gave vent to it thus : —

> "No grape that's kindly ripe could be
> So round, so plump, so soft as she,
> Nor half so full of juice."

No wonder that it has been a persistent dream of masculine poets to —

> "Journey along
> With an armful of girl and a heart full of song!"

We older folk, who were brought up and educated in the sweet provincial ways, can see that it has been the atrabilious old maids and the matronly flirts who have banished the dear, delicious girl from artistic consideration. The woman of thirty, and upwards, by persistent manœuvring, has got between us and sweet sixteen. What we have to show for the change is the feminine novel of nasty morals. Of course many of these flabby romances about over-mature heroines are written by men; but they are mostly men of a beardless style with much complaint to make against their ancestors. A sound man naturally loves a healthy young girl and wants to be her father, her brother, or her lover, according to propriety. He is, moreover, lenient towards the elderly unmarried females, when they do not insist upon the superiority of an Isabella-colored complexion; but at best they are not girls; in which they differ from happily married women, who keep to themselves a girlish charm late into life.

We all have our misfortunes for which we are not in the least to blame. The single woman whose bloom is gone is interesting as an embodied pathos, but not thrilling as a sweetheart; she looks dry as a heroine of romance; she spoils a love-song. No wonder that the realists cannot fit their art to girlhood while their theory of life excludes sweetness and health. It is a pursuit of love within discouraging limitations when some middle-aged man, with gray in his whiskers, limps rheumatically on the track of a stout lady in her thirties, and with a picture of such a race is pessimism best represented.

But the healthy and natural girl, apple-cheeked and merry-eyed, sweet-voiced — πάρθενον ἀδύφονον — a girl of girls, is what charms mankind in life and literature. Her ways are like thistledown in a summer breeze; they suggest idyllic dreams and make us believe in all manner of delightful human happiness. We are all poets when she engages our imagination; we are all young when she loves us; we are all good in her presence, — holy-minded at thought of her.

Perhaps the surest sign of decadence in art is the appearance of the dame in the space naturally occupied by the lass; for it proves that taste is no longer an elemental impulse, but rather a matter of fashion, or of illicit influence. We do not find Madame Bovary appealing to the ever-fresh wells of our manhood. We could not be glad of having her for mother, wife, daughter, sister, or sweetheart. She poisons our imagination and repels our interest. It is a delight to turn away from her to the blushing young heroine who loves purely and with all her heart, — a girl as fresh and sound as a May strawberry.

Of all unnatural things none can seem quite so unjust as ill health falling upon a girl. Balzac, in one of his hideously interesting romances, pictures to the minutest line a poor child stricken with disease and robbed of her season of bud and bloom. I have always felt that the story was an unpardonable piece of writing. We sometimes see such pitiful and appealing objects in the street, or at some country place; but why should they be put into books written for our delectation?

Once upon a time a friend and I, upon archery intent, tramped together for a fortnight among the hills of North Carolina, in a region given over to the race of mountaineers. It was saddening to observe the lean, vacant, bloodless faces of the girls in the cabins. As a rule, however, activity of body and a certain limberness go with these desiccated-looking countenances, and now and again you find a flower of rustic loveliness wasting its sweetness and ignorance on the mountain air. An instance comes to mind. We were having luncheon at a spring under the hill, upon which an ancient cabin nestled amid its peach-trees.

Down a zig-zag path worn into the brick-yellow clay and rotten slate of the declivity came a maiden bearing on her head a cedar noggin. She stepped briskly and nimbly, not deigning to touch the noggin with her hand, but with scarcely perceptible head-movements kept it at perfect equilibrium on her crown. Barefooted, her coarse blue petticoat very scant and short, a wonderful brush of pale gold hair crinkling over her perfect shoulders, her arms half bare, a throat like a bird's, and a face-flower full of happy lights, she made just that sudden impression of æsthetic surprise which comes with the poet's rarest phrase and most unexpected rhyme.

It turned out that this strong young thing was as ignorant and empty as she was beautiful and healthy; but when she spoke to us her voice had the *timbre* of a hermit thrush's and she gave us a glimpse of teeth incomparably white and even. She was not timid, not bold, but natural. Took hold of my yew bow, which rested against a tree, and inquired about it, fingered my arrows and quiver, asked my companion whither we were going. All this time the cedar noggin on her sunny head wagged gently, but kept its place, until presently she took it off, and, with a melodious souse in the spring, filled it, replaced it aloft and walked back up the hill, hands down and absolutely sure of foot.

"Well," said my companion, in a breathless tone, "if I did n't think for a moment that you meant to shoot her! A regular wood nymph."

As for myself I did not like the term wood nymph applied to a girl like that. She was as pretty, as pure, and as ignorant as a wild blue violet, and evidently as happy as a lark in a meadow. I felt the better for having seen her, and, as we trudged on, there was a new fragrance in my imagination.

The streets and suburban lanes of our little Western towns and cities offer great facilities for the study of happy girlhood, large thanks to the bicycle. During my summer walks and drives I meet whisps and flocks and bevies of lasses, or they pass me at scorching speed. They put the "bicycle-face" to shame with their rippling countenances and merry chatter. I shall never, I hope, forget one little maid of fifteen who drove her wheel as straight and steady as a flying quail, with her arms folded on her breast, and her lithe body poised inimitably. She looked at me with big round eyes, as if to say : "Do you see how I can do this?"

Indeed, my enjoyment of the frank sweetness in the air where girls are at play would be perfect were it not for the "Little Lord Fauntleroy" so often in evidence; but for him, all becurled and beruffled, I have a supreme and stony aversion. If some ruddy, ragged urchin, of the true Adamic race, would but down him and bedaub him with mud! If some girl would spank him and send him home; but the girl seems actually to like the self-conscious and unnatural little scamp. She smoothes his collar and pulls down his velvet jacket, hugs him and calls him pet names. He is the fellow who will grow up to be gun-shy, and inclined to marry a double-divorced actress, much to the girl's disgust.

It was Madame de Staël, I believe, who said: "Let my children be not girls; for a woman's life is so sad." Even she, however, did not find girlhood unhappy, and the preventive to be used against the misery of womanhood would be to hold on to girlish simplicity, faith, and sanity as long as possible. We grow like what we contemplate, and the question is, do we now-a-days give adequate contemplation to the true, the beautiful, and the good, whose symbol and measure is the heart of a healthy girl? Our civilization must luxuriate in what maidenhood can safely assimilate, or it must grovel at the feet of the yellow woman, tough and *passée*.

There is encouraging evidence, visible just now, of a desire on the public's part to get rid of Old Mrs. Woman, and take up once more with her granddaughter, the not wholly unsophisticated, but yet quite innocent and undesigning maiden. Men of the right sort have always felt that the happy married woman should be sheltered from publicity, and that the unhappy wife's sorrows are sacred; but the love of a youth and a maid, that is something for the delight of the whole world. We are tired of this rank immorality tricked out in the toggery of love, — and the lovers married to other folk, — this rank immorality of the old blasé hero and the adroit, conscienceless and time-battered heroine.

A return to the insipid pastoral of the early centuries would be tolerable, if no better shift can be had, as breach full and wide with the feminine party of faded spinsterhood and preposterous sociology, of tirades against marriage and of the sainthood of grass widows. Let in the young girl of sound body and merry heart; give her another chance; the whole world is ready to welcome her. Her smile will banish the yellow dust of the faded asters; her presence will hush even the whisper of brutalities.

The other day I wrote to a distant friend and put to him Horace's light question: —

"Quæ circumvolitas agilis thyma?"

Back came the answer: "I am running races with my three little girls. What is there better to do?" A man of gravity and distinction playing with his little daughters has what a politician would call a "pull" upon the gods for the highest joy of existence. From that play-ground he bears away the nectar of incomparable flowers, and the pollen on his thighs will freshen the whole hive of the world.

We may be sure that there is something wrong when we hear it growled around that young maidenhood is insipid in art, and that virility — a murrain seize the word — demands a Harriet Martineau, or the like, for a good, substantial feast of the imagination. Not assuming to know a great deal about virile women, I can venture the statement that truly virile men adore the young girl. She is the heroine of the iron-willed, vastly capable, boy-hearted fellows who make the world move. There is always a love of simple, elemental pleasures in great masculine natures. Precious little they care for artificial cheeks and pencilled eyebrows. Better a healthy, dewy-lipped milkmaid, singing behind the hedge, than a bediamonded old heiress whose teeth have ground luxuries some three dozen long years.

At all events my own preference for the blushing young heroine is unalterable, and I am eager to see her come back, garlanded and happy, to take her rightful place in both life and romance. I long to read yet one more book wherein the sound-hearted story-teller gives full run to that quintessential joy of loving which only the young girl can inspire. I am tired of bacon and potatoes; give me some of old Gervase Markham's simples —

> "The king-cup, the pansy with the violet,
> The rose that loves the shower,
> The wholesome gilliflower."

The Art of Saying Nothing
   Well
By
Maurice Thompson

THE ART OF SAYING NOTHING WELL

La simplicité divine de la pensée et du style.
— Paul Verlaine.

IN our day, as it now flies, there are fine films of distinction to be considered, notably in literary art. The merest gossamer of verbal indication must be respected in the behalf of style, lest a shade of meaning, no matter how vague, be lost from paragraph or phrase. The thing to be said is of no importance, we are told; but how it is said, that is the great matter.

If the title of the present paper be seriously studied it will prove puzzling to the average critic. It is a charming sentence, rich in possibilities of meaning. The last two words, like the tail of a bee, bear honey and poison on the same spike, or in sacs close by. Which shall you receive, a sweet drop or an enraging prick? What, indeed, does "saying nothing" mean? And nothing well said, does that mean a well-said nothing? or shall we understand that anything has been poorly said?

Behold how easily a pen slips into hopeless obscurities of mere ink! I see that I am gone wool-gathering, and that my verbal distinctions just attempted do not distinguish. Was it Horace who said this? —

"Non in caro nidore voluptas summa, sed in te ipso est."

The "precious smack," however, goes a long ways when there is nothing else to be had. The art of saying nothing well is the art of the bore or the art of the decadent, as you may interpret it. But a voice at my elbow quietly suggests that the distinction is still without a difference. The decadent, being always a bore, whether he has a precious smack or a smack of preciousness, has the art of saying nothing well and everything ill.

The good old days, when men who wrote were impressed with the value of original thought, were hard on brains, but easy on dictionaries. A tremendous idea was set for all time in a few words grabbed at random from a scant vocabulary. Even after "art for art's sake" had come to stay, the

CHAP-BOOK ESSAYS

By Maurice Thompson

great early poets were stingy in their verbal dealings with art. It is surprising to note how meagre is the vocabulary of Sappho, or of Theocritus, or of Pindar. And yet what incomparable riches of expression ! The masters were in a flux of imagination, and to them a word had no value beyond its fitness to stand as a perfect sign of what the brain originated. But not so with us ; we chase the word for the word's sake. We imagine that there is something precious in verbal style quite independent of what it may be used upon. A cheese, although rotten, is made sweet enough, we think, by being wrapped in an artistic poster.

We are quite familiar with the phase "good literature," which has come to mean nothing and that wordy, or a good thing and that well written, according to the individual taste of the critic deciding the matter. But most generally we now take for granted that there is really nothing worth saying on account of its intrinsic value. As a new woman said of her kind the other day, "Oh, the female form is but a clothes-horse nowadays. A woman is suggested, not seen, by what she wears," we may well say of thought : it is a mere word-rack, a peg upon which to hang attractive diction. Not unfrequently the thought is quite dispensed with and the phrasing hangs upon nothing.

If you have nothing to write, of course write it well. Good literature, like Homer's and Chaucer's and Shakespeare's, was well enough before Théophile Gautier invented style; but since then there has come a change, and now we demand, not new matter, but always a new manner. As for durability, we are satisfied with a season's run; permanency is not desirable. Fame, which once was a thing to die for, has taken on the form of a spring jacket or summer cravat; you wear it till the next change in the weather. The art of saying nothing well is as fickle as the moon; for nothing and woman pride themselves upon varying their fashions; and what is good literature now but woman and nothing? Aminta and her George Meredith strut before us as if they owned the earth; but tomorrow there will be another woman and a new nothing.

The happiest literary folk in all the world must be those in Paris, who actually took Paul Verlaine seriously, and are now making obeisance to Stéphane

Mallarme. They seem to be, if we leave out certain provençal dialect writers and our own American critics, the only *litterateurs* upon earth who would heroically die rather than be right. M. Mallarmé expresses perfectly in a single phrase the whole ambition of his literary flock: "d'abord et toujours et irrésistiblement Verlaine." But how charming a thing literature is in the hands of these *poêtes maudits*, as Verlaine styled them! To be sure, it is naught but nothing well said. Verlaine may have been right when he wrote his eulogy: "Absolus par l'imagination, absolus par l'expression, absolus comme les Reys Netos des meilleurs siècles;" there is much to be said about nothing, and more about such writers as Corbière, Rimbaud, Mallarmé, and Villiers de L'Isle-Adam, who have served to amuse a blasé crowd of the best fellows that ever lived, the Alexandrian Greek poets doubtfully excepted.

What Sir Walter Scott called "the big bow-wow" is not suited to the perfect expression of nothing. Browning's diction gets on better at a pinch, when the poet has to resort to a dazzling display of blank verbal cartridges; for sometimes it is almost impossible to distinguish a meaningless whiff of word-wind from a whizzing bullet of thought. We dodge with delight when either clips too near us. The other day I was auditing the book-bills of "Narcissus," and found myself delicately and deliciously charmed by what under different circumstances would have been a mere lack of assets to back the paper. Style never went further nor came back with a more fragrant and savory load of nothing. From paragraph to paragraph one glides over a meandering smoothness. It is like bicycling on imaginary asphalt between immaterial clover fields. One hears bumblebees and sheep and kine; but never is there any visible or tangible matter of delectation: only a lulling composite noise; *vox et præterea nihil.* This voice of the hollow sphere and this dripping of melodious word-showers, to change the figures, combine to high perfection in the latest good literature. Think of what a fascination a style can have, when a young girl fresh from Vassar flings down a volume by William Sharp, or one by I. Zangwill, and rapturously exclaims: "Shakespeare and Scott are not in it for a minute longer!" How delightful to do good that evil may come!

It would be hardly fair to wring into this paper a

CHAP-BOOK ESSAYS

By Maurice Thompson

consideration of the art of writing nothing ill. Walt Whitman and Stephen Crane have given practical demonstrations of what may be done at a venture in that field. Here again my own style persists in obscurity. Nothing to write and the poorest imaginable style, is not exactly the same with plenty to write and not a sentence ill written. The art of writing nothing and writing it ill might, however, be admirable in the hands of a master. For example, there is Andrew Lang's eulogy of H. Rider Haggard's stories, which I might cite in any part of this essay with perfect propriety and unqualified approval, as being strictly in point. When Mr. Lang has absolutely nothing for subject he is alluringly objective and revels in good literature. He is singularly expert in writing nothing ill.

But the art of writing nothing well, of writing so that nothing is well said, or whatever I mean, offers difficulties not readily foreseen by the ambitious candidate for authorhood. Nothing must ever be dressed up to look like a great something with an honorable ancestry and a congenital lease upon posterity, unless we accept the other interpretation of my caption. What could, on the other hand, be reasonably described as the bloomer-costume style of writing, by which effeminate imaginings are made to masquerade as virile and of the major origin, demands serious and exhaustive study. To achieve it William Watson has, we hope, a long life of self-reform before him; but some are born to it. Austin Dobson would not, apparently, give a penny to have it, albeit some of his best work neatly grazes the goal. Happy accident has done much on this score for Henry James, reading whose latest work one might exclaim with Mr. Sherburne Hardy: "But yet a woman!" And Mr. Howells should never go near a Shaker village if he has any regard for what old friends think of his style. It makes him say nothing with unusual delight.

When I get back to my Greek, as I usually do at the earliest moment, an essay like Aristotle's on poetry makes me wonder how it has lived so long and kept so well, seeing that it says something without regard, at any point, to "lightness of touch" or to preciousness of phrasing. It is not good literature, measured by the standard of Robert Louis Stevenson's style; but in its gnarls of diction are thoughts hard bound with fibres that are indestructible. Aristotle was too busy inside of his brain to have much respect for exterior frills; but where shall we find solider phrases than he snatched out of his stinted vocabulary? It is tough reading, almost as bad as Browning's best, and the words grate together like teeth with sand between them; still, something is said. You remember his turns of diction by associating them with his thoughts; but you never dream of regarding him as a writer with a style-charm. His fascination comes from deep down, as if sent up by roots squeezed between bowlders.

And it is true that a permanent fascination of style is always due to something more than nothing well said. The attempt has been made in American criticism to stow a poem like Poe's "Raven" away in the lumber garret as a mere word-trick; but there is something tremendously human in the spiritual adumbration by which that great poem sustains itself. Style is there, superb style; and the clutch of grim sorrow, the pang of despair, and the helplessness of a soul in the presence of fate, are there as well. Poe could not command Stevenson's nimble diction, nor could he even understand what humor like Lowell's was. The power in his work came from behind his lines out of a wellspring hidden in a strange and original mind. He "played with dictionaries" and feigned abstruse learning; but he said new and impressive things in a new and impressive style.

The deepest truth connected with the permanency of art is that there must be style, which does not stand for the same thing as diction, nor for the same thing as characteristic stroke, manner, or tone. Mere deftness with the brush, mere cleverness with the fiddle-bow, mere facility in the doing of word-jugglery, cannot pass into permanent art, and this is the lesson we need to-day. We take verbal style too seriously when we reckon with it as of more importance than fresh thought and enlarged ideals. It is not the art of saying nothing well that wins in the long run; it is the art of saying a great thing with a simple charm of style which does most to enrich literature. Indeed, great things are themselves simple, the greatest the simplest. Nothing is well said when nothing is said.

THE END

PRINTED AT THE LAKESIDE PRESS
FOR HERBERT S. STONE & CO.
PUBLISHERS, CHICAGO

October, 1896.   *Established May, 1896.*   Number 1.

Catalogue
of
The Publications
of
Herbert S. Stone & Company
The Caxton Building,
Chicago.

To be had of all Booksellers, or will be sent postpaid on receipt of price by the Publishers.

HENRY JAMES.
WHAT MAISIE KNEW; a novelette. 16mo. $1.25.

The announcement of a new book by Mr. James is in itself an event of no slight literary importance. The present volume represents his latest work and is worthy the attention of all persons interested in English and American letters.

RICHARD Le GALLIENNE.

PROSE FANCIES; second series, by the author of "The Book-bills of Narcissus," etc., with a cover designed by Frank Hazenplug. 16mo. $1.25.

"In these days of Beardsley pictures and decadent novels, it is good to find a book as sweet, as pure, as delicate as Mr. Le Gallienne's."—NEW ORLEANS PICAYUNE.

"PROSE FANCIES ought to be in everyone's summer library, for it is just the kind of a book one loves to take to some secluded spot to read and dream over."—KANSAS CITY TIMES.

"There are witty bits of sayings by the score, and sometimes whole paragraphs of nothing but wit. Somewhere there is a little skit about 'Scotland, the country that takes its name from the whisky made there,' and the transposed proverb like : 'It is an ill wind for the shorn lamb,' and 'Many rise on the stepping stones of their dead relations,' are brilliant. 'Most of us would never be heard of were it not for our enemies,' is a capital epigram."—CHICAGO TIMES-HERALD.

"Mr. Le Gallienne is first of all a poet, and these little essays, which savor somewhat of Lamb, of Montaigne, of Lang, and of Birrell, are larded with verse of exquisite grace. He rarely ventures into the grotesque, but his fancy follows fair paths ; a certain quaintness of expression and the idyllic atmosphere of the book charm one at the beginning and carry one through the nineteen 'fancies' that comprise the volume."—CHICAGO RECORD.

MARIA LOUISE POOL.

IN BUNCOMBE COUNTY. 16mo. $1.25.

A volume of connected sketches of country life in the South. It is on the order of Miss Pool's recent book entitled "In a Dike Shanty" which received such favorable comment. It is not sensational ; it is not exciting ; it is merely peaceful and pleasing, with a quiet current of delightful humor running all through.

MARTIN J. PRITCHARD.
WITHOUT SIN; a novel. 12mo. $1.25.
Second edition.

The NEW YORK JOURNAL gave a half-page review of the book and proclaimed it "the most startling novel yet."

"Abounds in situations of thrilling interest. A unique and daring book."—REVIEW OF REVIEWS (London).

"One is hardly likely to go far wrong in predicting that WITHOUT SIN will attract abundant notice. Too much can scarcely be said in praise of Mr. Pritchard's treatment of his subject."— ACADEMY (London).

"The very ingenious way in which improbable incidents are made to appear natural, the ingenious manner in which the story is sustained to the end, the undoubted fascination of the writing, and the convincing charm of the principal characters, are just what make this novel so deeply dangerous while so intensely interesting."—THE WORLD (London).

CHAP-BOOK STORIES; a volume of Reprints from the Chap-Book, by OCTAVE THANET, GRACE ELLERY CHANNING, MARIA LOUISE POOL, AND OTHERS. 16mo. $1.25.

The authors of this volume are all American. Beside the well-known names, there are some which were seen in the Chap-Book for the first time. The volume is bound in an entirely new and startling fashion.

CHAP-BOOK ESSAYS, by T. W. HIGGINSON, LOUISE CHANDLER MOULTON, H. H. BOYESEN, H. W. MABIE, AND OTHERS. 16mo. $1.25.

Essays, by the most distinguished living writers, which it has been judged worth preserving in more permanent form than the issues of the Chap-Book could give.

ALBERT KINROSS.

THE FEARSOME ISLAND; being a Modern rendering of the narrative of one Silas Fordred, Master Mariner of Hythe, whose shipwreck and subsequent adventures are herein set forth. Also an appendix accounting in a rational manner for the seeming marvels that Silas Fordred encountered during his sojourn on the fearsome island of Don Diego Rodriguez. With a cover designed by Frank Hazenplug. 16mo. $1.25.

GABRIELE D'ANNUNZIO.

EPISCOPO AND COMPANY. Translated by Myrta Leonora Jones. 16mo. $1.25.

Gabriele d'Annunzio is the best known and most gifted of modern Italian novelists. His work is making a great sensation at present in all literary circles. The translation now offered gives the first opportunity English-speaking readers have had to know him in their own language.

ARTHUR MORRISON.

A CHILD OF THE JAGO; a novel of the East End of London, by the author of "Tales of Mean Streets." 12mo. $1.50.

Mr. Morrison is recognized the world over as the most capable man at slum life stories. His "Tales of Mean Streets" was one of the best received books of 1894-95, and the present volume has occupied his time ever since. It is of great force and continuous interest; a book that, once begun, must be finished, and one that will figure as a sensation for a long time to come.

JULIA MAGRUDER.
MISS AYR OF VIRGINIA AND OTHER STORIES. 16mo. $1.25.

Critics have always united in saying of Miss Magruder's work that it was interesting. In addition to this her new volume is noticeable for its grace and beauty, real sentiment where it is needed, and strength as well. It will be welcomed by the many who enjoyed "The Princess Sonia" and "The Violet."

HENRY M. BLOSSOM, Jr.
CHECKERS; a Hard-Luck Story, by the author of "The Documents in Evidence." 16mo. $1.25. Third edition.

" Abounds in the most racy and picturesque slang."— N. Y. RECORDER.

"CHECKERS is an interesting and entertaining chap, a distinct type, with a separate tongue and a way of saying things that is oddly humorous."—CHICAGO RECORD.

"If I had to ride from New York to Chicago on a slow train, I should like half a dozen books as gladsome as CHECKERS, and I could laugh at the trip."—N. Y. COMMERCIAL ADVERTISER.

ALICE MORSE EARLE.
CURIOUS PUNISHMENTS OF BYGONE DAYS; by the author of "Sabbath in Puritan New England," etc., with many quaint pictures by Frank Hazenplug. 12mo. $1.50.

Mrs. Earle dedicates her book, in the language of an old-time writer, to "All curious and ingenious gentlemen and gentlewomen who can gain from acts of the past a delight in the present days of virtue, wisdom and the humanities."

H. C. CHATFIELD-TAYLOR.

THE LAND OF THE CASTANET; Spanish Sketches, by the author of "Two Women and a Fool," with twenty-five full-page illustrations. 16mo. $1.25.

A collection of rambling sketches of Spanish people and places. Mr. Chatfield-Taylor has written frankly and entertainingly of the most striking features of "The Land of the Castanet." The volume does not pretend to be exhaustive; in no sense is it a guide book—it is intended rather for the person who does not expect to visit Spain than for the traveller.

C. E. RAIMOND.

THE FATAL GIFT OF BEAUTY AND OTHER STORIES, by the author of "George Mandeville's Husband," etc. 16mo. $1.25.

A book of stories which will not quickly be surpassed for real humor, skillful characterization and splendid entertainment. "The Confessions of a Cruel Mistress" is a masterpiece and the "Portman Memmoirs" are exceptionally clever.

GEORGE ADE.

ARTIE; a story of the Streets and Town, with many pictures by John T. McCutcheon. 16mo. $1.25.

These sketches, reprinted from the CHICAGO RECORD, attracted great attention on their original appearance. They have been revised and rewritten and in their present form promise to make one of the most popular books of the fall.

LUCAS MALET.

THE CARISSIMA; a novel, by the author of "The Wages of Sin." 12mo. $1.50.

Few people will have difficulty in remembering the profound sensation which the publication of "The Wages of Sin" caused some six years ago. Since that time Lucas Malet has published no serious work, and the present volume therefore, represents her best. It is a novel of intense and continued interest, and will claim a prominent place among the books of the season.

ALSO

THE CHAP-BOOK.

WHAT IT STANDS FOR.

"The cleverness of this periodical has always amply justified its existence but the careless reader, who has never taken it seriously, will be surprised to find on turning over the leaves of this volume how very much more than merely clever it is. It contains examples of some of the strongest work that is now being done in letters. It represents the best tendencies of the younger writers of the day, and, seen in bulk, even its freaks and excentricities are shown to be representative of their sort, and are present in it because they are representative, and not because they are freakish."—St. Paul Globe.

Price, 10 Cents. $2.00 A Year.

Published by HERBERT S. STONE & CO., Chicago.

Herbert S. Stone & Company,
THE CHAP-BOOK.

CHICAGO: The Caxton Building.

LONDON: 10, Norfolk St., Strand.

TELEGRAPHIC ADDRESSES:

"CHAPBOOK, CHICAGO."

"EDITORSHIP, LONDON."

www.ingramcontent.com/pod-product-compliance
Lightning Source LLC
Chambersburg PA
CBHW031943230426
43672CB00010B/2033